BEFORE THE INVENTION
OF PARADISE
VOR DERERFINDUNGDESPARADIESES

Ludwig Steinherr
BEFORE THE INVENTION OF PARADISE

VOR DER ERFINDUNG DES PARADIESES

❦

Translated by
Richard Dove

Introduced by Jean Boase-Beier

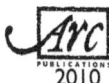

Arc
PUBLICATIONS
2010

Published by Arc Publications,
Nanholme Mill, Shaw Wood Road
Todmorden OL14 6DA, UK

Original poems copyright © Ludwig Steinherr 2010
Translation copyright © Richard Dove 2010
Preface copyright © Richard Dove 2010
Introduction copyright © Jean Boase-Beier 2010

Design by Tony Ward
Printed and bound by Lightning Source

978 1904614 45 6 (pbk)

ACKNOWLEDGEMENTS
The poems in this volume have been selected from: *Fluganweisung*
(Munich: Schneekluth, 1985), *Unsre Gespräche bis in den Morgen*
(Eisingen: Heiderhoff, 1991), *Vor der Erfindung des Paradieses*
(Eisingen: Heiderhoff, 1993), *Buchstäbliches Blau* (Munich: Kro-
nenbitter, 1994), *Erste Blicke, letzte Blicke* (Eisingen: Heiderhoff,
1996), *Musikstunde bei Vermeer* (Eisingen: Heiderhoff, 1998),
Fresko, vielfach übermalt (Munich: Lyrikedition, 2002), *Hinter
den Worten die Brandung* (Munich: Lyrikedition, 2003), *Vor aller
Zeit* (Hauzenberg: Pongratz, 2003), *Die Hand im Feuer* (Munich:
Lyrikedition 2005).

Cover photograph: "Vertreibung aus dem Paradies" (Expulsion
from Paradise) – panel dated 1015 on a bronze door in
Hildesheim Cathedral. Reproduced by kind
permission of Dom-Museum Hildesheim
(photograph: © Frank Tomio).

Supported by
**ARTS COUNCIL
ENGLAND**

Arc Publications 'Visible Poets' series
Editor: Jean Boase-Beier

CONTENTS

SERIES EDITOR'S NOTE

The 'Visible Poets' series was established in 2000, and set out to challenge the view that translated poetry could or should be read without regard to the process of translation it had undergone. Since then, things have moved on. Today there is more translated poetry available and more debate on its nature, its status, and its relation to its original. We know that translated poetry is neither English poetry that has mysteriously arisen from a hidden foreign source, nor is it foreign poetry that has silently rewritten itself in English. We are more aware that translation lies at the heart of all our cultural exchange; without it, we must remain artistically and intellectually insular.

One of the aims of the series was, and still is, to enrich our poetry with the very best work that has appeared elsewhere in the world. And the poetry-reading public is now more aware than it was at the start of this century that translation cannot simply be done by anyone with two languages. The translation of poetry is a creative act, and translated poetry stands or falls on the strength of the poet-translator's art. For this reason 'Visible Poets' publishes only the work of the best translators, and gives each of them space, in a Preface, to talk about the trials and pleasures of their work.

From the start, 'Visible Poets' books have been bilingual. Many readers will not speak the languages of the original poetry but they, too, are invited to compare the look and shape of the English poems with the originals. Those who can are encouraged to read both. Translation and original are presented side-by-side because translations do not displace the originals; they shed new light on them and are in turn themselves illuminated by the presence of their source poems. By drawing the readers' attention to the act of translation itself, it is the aim of these books to make the work of both the original poets and their translators more visible.

Jean Boase-Beier

Peaceful breath

For a long time I watch
the archer
there at the end of the square

Motionless, concentrated
he stands there

his taut bow
(a precision instrument)
aimed at the
very distant target –

impossible to decide
if that even, peaceful breath
belongs to someone meditating

or to
a marksman

It was poems like this one, from Ludwig Steinherr's remarkably assured debut collection, published in 1985 when he was just 23, which first attracted my attention. I had moved to Munich in 1987, at a time when German poetry was going through a decidedly feeble phase before the emergence of compelling new voices such as Draesner's or Grünbein's or Kling's, and here was a young writer whose poems seemed inevitable. By chance, I met him in the following autumn at a colloquium for young poets from West and East Germany, sponsored by IBM Deutschland, and mentioned that I was keen to translate some of his work. What I did not know then was what was to come – nine collections in the intervening seventeen years which have worked out the implications of that debut in an inspired fashion. Steinherr sent me a copy of each book as soon as it appeared, and each time translation proved the best way of coming to terms with his new departures.

Translating is a decidedly meditative activity, and so it is often difficult for the translator to account at a later date for the many little decisions that are made automatically while the trance lasts. I can often only tell from the versions scribbled and hastily revised in the margins of the collections what revision process, if any, has taken place. One case in point might be the painful lines in 'Homo sapiens': "The men in jack-boots / their [mechanical / metallic / industrial / *not* industrious / cavernous laughter] booming guffaws" (p.105). When the process did become conscious, I was guided by several more abstract principles.

First, that the English should be more or less in line with the idiolect with which I grew up: hence colloquialisms such as "what you're on about" or "as though I'd gone / and ruined my eyes". An extension of this principle was to permit a certain degree of licence if it made for a text which sounded "right" in English: the beloved's single hair quivering "in the *storm* of my / breath" ('Black night') is an attempt to bring out the tempestuousness which remains decorously latent in the original, "beneath my breath" (p. 95).

Second, that deliberate borrowings from tradition should not be suppressed if they assert themselves insistently enough. The translator, like the original poet, is not immune to intertextuality. Hence "failure's a doctrine like any other", in 'Wisdoms for moderate climates', distantly echoes Sylvia Plath's traumatic line "Dying is an art, like everything else" ('Lady Lazarus'), whereas the original – literally "Failure is a doctrine" – is more elliptical in the customary German manner (p.111). The "great tradition" conjured up in 'Death of the painter' (p. 85) ironically alludes to F. R. Leavis's rather portentous book-title of the same name. The formulation "lovers in one another's arms" partly replicates a line from Yeats's 'Sailing to Byzantium' ("The young / In one another's arms"), because it seemed to fit the context but also because it helped to complete the rhythmic contour (p. 75). The "dying fall" in 'Finis operis' (p. 67) was, at some submerged level, an obeisance to T. S. Eliot ('The Love Song of J. Alfred Prufrock'). And "the desert of silence" (p. 77) in 'The temptation of St. Anthony', which in the end seemed more appropriate than a more literal reading like "the utter silence", is clearly in the debt of Andrew Marvell's "vast deserts of eternity" ('To His Coy Mistress'). Over and above this, one's practice as a translator is (perhaps inevitably) coloured by the habits picked up *sur le motif* while writing one's own poetry: the slant rhyme which closes 'Palaeontological museum' – "a beast / at rest" (rather than "a resting / animal", the original formulation) – is one example, owed in turn to the precedent of Wilfred Owen and the late Yeats (p. 105).

Third, that the translations (without in any way seeking to smooth over the inevitable foreignness of their originals) should be assimilative – in the specific sense that it is their job to render anything that would otherwise make a merely outlandish impression into terms which are more readily intelligible in the host language. Accordingly, "Müdigkeit der Worte", which (being elliptical) would have an almost liturgical ring if conveyed literally ("weariness of words"), gets explicated: "the weariness at the heart of words" (p. 65). By the same token, "Orphische Urworte" (literally "primeval orphic words"), an allusion to a late poem by Goethe, ends up being translated into what Northrop Frye called the "low mimetic", i.e. into the rather more down-to earth exclamation "it's orphic" (p. 143). Ludwig Thoma, the late nineteenth-century Bavarian writer mentioned in the original of 'Changing trains', is so little known in the Anglo-Saxon world that dragging him onto the stage could easily have distracted attention from the murderous thrust of the poem in question (p. 113). The implications of an idiom like "die Hand ins Feuer legen" (literally "to put one's hand in the fire", i.e. to vouch for somebody or something), which constitutes the axis on which the title poem of Steinherr's 2005 volume turns, similarly required being made more explicit: "as Scaevola did" (p. 133).

Not that the latter principle could be applied mechan-istically – there were times when a ruthlessly alienating translation seemed the only option. In 'Nada', for instance, Heid-egger's monosyllabic "Nichts" has been kept at the expense of the polysyllabic translation "Nothingness" because the brevity of the German term is a central part of the poem's point (p. 33).

And an alienation effect was particularly necessary in the case of 'Why are you surprised…': a literal translation, "Nation", would have had an upbeat nation-building ring; it had to be "Volk", a term with unmistakably racist connotations (p. 113).

A special problem was posed by the four ghazals (pp. 78, 84, 86, and 116). Steinherr, who is a virtuoso when it comes to reproducing special effects in translations of other people's rhymed poems,[1] has conspicuously refrained from using rhyme in his own work, perhaps because such ornament would deflect attention from the seriousness of its quest. The exception here is only half an exception: the occasional ghazals which he has written ever since his debut collection. Half an exception because the rhymes in this old Persian form revived in Germany by late romantic poets like Rückert and Platen (rhymes which materialise in the opening two lines and subsequently in every second line, regardless of the poem's length) are largely counteracted by the rhymeless lines which intervene, creating – on balance – a kind of *chiascuro* effect: brightness very nearly outweighed by darkness. The danger lying in wait for the translator here is, of course, what the Germans call *Reimzwang* – the compulsion to rhyme even if one is led further and further away from the original in the process. As far as I can see, master translators like Michael Hamburger or Christopher Middleton are never prepared to stretch or maim the intrinsic sense on the Procrustes bed of form.[2] But in this particular predicament my conclusion was that rhymeless versions of these central poems would somehow sell my author short. In each case, I started with a kind of framework, composed of strings of rhymes and off-rhymes that had been generated using what could perhaps be styled a random algorithm. The copy of my collection of *Fresko, vielfach übermalt* reminds me that

---

[1] *cf.* Steinherr's German translations of recent poems by Michael Hamburger, collected in M. Hamburger, *Unterhaltung mit der Muse des Alters*, Munich, 2004.

[2] Michael Hamburger dispenses with rhyme, for example, in his version of Loerke's 'Berliner Winterabend', giving his translation coherence through the suggestive use of (broken) iambic pentameters; the one rhyme, "wind" / "blind", straightforward in German but paradoxically a "blind" eye-rhyme in English, is all the more stark as a result when one stumbles across it (M. Hamburger, *German Poetry 1910-1975*, Manchester 1977, p.45). Christopher Middleton's version of Mörike's 'Auf eine Lampe' expertly harnesses the iambic trimeters that had been pressed into service in the German original but then refuses to ride them dogmatically to death (C. Middleton, *Faint Harps and Silver Voices. Selected Translations*, Manchester 2000, p.77).

the version of 'Vermeer' (p. 85) was drafted during a longish trip by ferry from Ancona to Patras on 4 August 2003. The starting point was the fortuitous paradigm-set "create / fate / gait / wait / hate / innate / sate / gate / relate / generate / pulsate / vibrate / detonate / concentrate", and the rough version set down on that not particularly rough passage read as follows:

VERMEER

[This] The silent world – how [arduous / difficult to create]
    hard to recreate.
The table – won't stand still. They all pulsate:
The jug, the cloth, the map up on the wall.
The golden nails sunk in the chair vibrate –
Can only just about keep it in place.
What light! Its particles [rave] [rush] stream and detonate,
Causing the [leaden pane / lead glass pane / pane of lead
    glass] leaded glass to almost [burst] crack!
[But the young woman] And yet the girl [at her music /
    playing music / whose unheard songs sound sweet]
    whose melodies sound sweet
[Does not] Doesn't turn round. The woman making lace
[Does not] Doesn't look up. [She has to] She's got to concentrate
To make sure that her threads don't [get ensnared / get
    entwined / don't snag] get confused.
[How easily things lose their heads, their weight! / How
    soon things lose their heads, once so sedate!]
How things freak out and start to resonate!

This – like the other versions of Steinherr's ghazals – can only aspire to be a transposition rather than a translation proper, once again proving the truth of the old Italian play *traddutore traditore*: to translate is to traduce.

Steinherr's poems are limpid, stripped down to essentials – an art of "reduction", to cite the recent meditation 'A poet dies', where the author is admittedly speaking not of his own achievement but of the monitor on which the last spasms of his dying friend are being dispassionately recorded (p. 119). As a result, the main challenge facing the translator is a negative one: to muddy these clear waters as little as possible. There is nothing soft or euphuistic about the way Steinherr formulates; the translator's task is to shrink back from embellishment and to attempt to match the precision, the hardness of touch in these originals sculpted by a man whose name, in German, just happens to mean stonemason:

PAIN

Hardest of all currencies
that's legal tender everywhere –

Universal language
in need of no translators […]

(p. 115)

Richard Dove

Ludwig Steinherr, in common with most poets in the 'Visible Poets' series, is still almost unknown in England. Yet his poetry, both profound and accessible, seems an obvious candidate for English translation. For one thing, it gives us a picture of the things that concern many modern German poets: its themes are silence, memory, knowing and the impossibility of knowing, the everyday and what is beyond. It also shares with much contemporary German poetry its spareness of style, lack of ornamentation and even of punctuation. This stylistic spareness, whose origins can partly be seen in the rejection of earlier poetic conventions, is also common to what is sometimes regarded as philosophical poetry.[1] This is the type of poetry sometimes criticised for lack of poetic imagery or rhythm (see for example Robert Minhinnick on R. S. Thomas[2]). Criticisms like this should not be seen merely as complaints about lack of embellishment; they are, rather, based on the idea that complexity of thought, form, and imagery must lie within the poem itself. As indeed it often does. We only have to think of the poetry of poets such as Hopkins or Rilke to realise that the style is intimately tied to an exquisite complexity of thought that demands similar work of its reader.

But there are different types of complexity. Steinherr can be compared with other modern German poets such as Ernst Meister or Sarah Kirsch, or non-German poets such as R. S. Thomas, in that he uses stylistic spareness as an opening for the reader. Think, for example, of the weight of questions that Thomas can place behind a word like "it". For the reader, pondering the reference of a simple pronoun leads to a consideration of different interpretations, not only of that word, that line, or that poem, but also of the concepts it might refer to, of the nature of those concepts, and so of religious teaching in general. In philosophical and religious poetry like Thomas's or Steinherr's, the complexity lies almost entirely in what is not said, for it is here that the

---

[1] A term used famously by Santayana, for example, in his 1953 book *Three Philosophical Poets* (New York: Doubleday).
[2] In *Poetry Wales* Vol. 29, No. 1, July 1993, pp. 11-14.

reader's thoughts must take over.

Another way to approach Steinherr's poetry is to see it in the context of a concern with everyday concrete detail, as in the work of earlier poets such as Walter Höllerer or Günter Eich or in Enzensberger and Günter Grass. It is a concern that culminates in, for example, Kirsch's use of everyday objects and processes (onions, ground coffee, gardening) and the way they open up a labyrinth in the reader's mind. Steinherr, like Kirsch, like Enzensberger, is very good at suggesting the complexity behind the everyday, the terror in the moment a photograph documents, the monster on the edge of a map ('Finding one's bearings', p. 25), the sudden glimpse of a tumour in 'Southern café' (p. 43).

And yet this poet seems to me different from his contemporaries in what we might call the positive slant of his ambiguity. Even while he shows us the skull beneath the skin, this 'bony shape' does not shock him (or us) into mindless terror, as we might expect, but instead into "unexpected tenderness" ('With a bag of fruit in the rain', p. 27). It is true that his poetry is full of what is just below the surface, pregnant with absences so marked that at times he reminds one of Thomas Hardy: like Hardy, he writes of the sentences in unsent letters ('Post delivered late', p. 137), of the absence of a lover ('Letter', p. 93), of an empty house ('After her husband's death', p. 123). And it is certainly the case that these silences in Steinherr also suggest the silences that have been described (for example by Ernestine Schlant in *The Language of Silence: West German Literature and the Holocaust,* 1999) as the "blind spots and absences" which reveal "unstated assumptions" (p. 3) or even "a refusal to become aware" (p. 7) in post-Holocaust writing. It is the silence of memory that cannot be expressed, that must not be forgotten: the heap of glasses or the wrenched-out fillings ('On Abstraction', p. 115).

But it is also, and strikingly so, the silence which leaves space for other voices to speak. Positive thought or necessary action can and must come out of failure, regret or disaster. A miracle happens where there is "a slight disappointment" ('The miracle', p. 41) or even in the presence of violence ('Miracle'); and it is deception which lets us see and value the truth ('Poems', p. 59). One has to be careful here, because it would be easy, interpreting

17

Steinherr's poetry in this way, to make him seem complacently positive. Yet he is the opposite. Life is inherently precarious. There is a poem in this collection which epitomises, for me, this knife-edge uncertainty of events: in 'Southern scene' (p. 47) two teenagers are throwing each other an open knife, suggestive of both the risks and the excitement of openness. In poetry, that openness is key, and Steinherr's poetry is very careful not to close off meaning by being too obvious. Images are ambiguous, poems end without a full stop, minimal punctuation leaves even the syntax open to question. Lexical items have more than one meaning: "in the end" ('In Life') can mean a final interpretation, a bottom line or the point of death. Absences that suggest what is to come or what might be to come ('In the moment...') are as important as those absences whose cause can be pinpointed in the past ('Letter', p. 93). Afterlife is as important as backstory. And so textual gaps, that play so important and poignant a role in modern German poetry, are here not just silent monuments for loss, but they are also the place for the reader to come in, to paraphrase Wolfgang Iser's famous expression.[3] Where the poet does not provide a ready answer, each reader must find her or his own. Where the poet is silent, the reader must speak. Though an everyday object is very much itself – a lizard or a tea-cup or a bag of fruit – it is also that which we think about it.

Thinking, for the philosopher, for the poet, and for all of us, is confirmation of life and protection from despair ('One can't' p. 23). But thought, like the open knife, can also be dangerous, because it can lead us to categorise into difference instead of see-ing commonality: those brutal images of the heap of glasses and the wrenched-out dental fillings return. Thought lurks behind trees and stones ('The innocence of stone', p. 29). It allows life, but also destruction. It is up to us.

Just as objects and events are open to a multitude of inter-pretations and consequences, so the poems are open to multiple

[3] See Iser, 'The Implied Reader: Patterns of Communication' in *Prose Fiction from Bunyan to Beckett* (Baltimore: Johns Hopkins University Press, 1974) p. 275.

interpretation and beyond this, to whatever actions might result. When such openness is so closely reflected in the various stylistic devices of the poetry, what does this mean for its translation?

Of course all poetry works by expressing ambiguity and leaving to the reader the various thoughts that can co-exist in the process of interpretation, and the translator must preserve that ambiguity or lose the cognitive effects of the poems. With Steinherr's poetry, preserving this ambiguity is paramount. He loves ambiguous images: a photograph captures (and loses) its object but it also implies the photographer, a lizard is scary and beautiful, blood is a symbol of life and of death. A tumour is cell-division gone mad. And the words themselves, with all their chains of meaning and connotation, are so careful. In the poem 'Markt, Abend' (p. 48), the ice is melting, 'rosig von Blut'. 'Rosig' suggests blood, but also dawn, health and a hopeful future. How important it is, then, that Dove preserves this epithet as 'rosy' in his English version 'Market, evening' (p. 49) . Or take the example of 'Lady Macbeth as a little girl' (pp. 50 / 51). The little girl "lauscht in die Dunkelheit", the accusative of the definite article *die* signalling that she does not listen "in" but "into" the dark, or, in Dove's evocative rendering, she "listens her way into the darkness". Just a small difference of case on the German definite article, but a world of difference in connotation. And using the word "darkness" rather than "dark" allows the translator to suggest the metaphorical darkness that plays so great a role in modern German history and literature. Dove is a translator, then, who is not only attuned to the connotations of every morpheme of his poet's words but is able to carry over these connotations while still leaving space for the reader to make meaning.

I am fascinated by the meticulousness of Dove's translations. I would often have done them differently myself, and this matters, in a very positive sense. For it points to an essential trait of good poetry: its openness to multiple reading and a multiplicity of translations. If poetry ever appears to have only one possible translation, it is not poetry. Steinherr's poetry makes you think, it makes you think different things at once and each time you read it. Dove's translation succeeds in two ways. That it works as English poetry will surprise no-one: Dove is himself an acclaimed poet. But to be a good translator it is not enough to be a good poet. You need the ability to identify and identify *with* the thought behind the written words of the poem, in order to bring over into the other language their gaps and openings for their new readers. You can read Dove's English versions alone or alongside the original poems: either way, you get that unique combination of the poet's and the translator's work that makes good translated poetry so rewarding.

Jean Boase-Beier

BEFORE THE INVENTION OF PARADISE

VOR DER ERFINDUNG DES PARADIESES

I

MAN KANN NICHT

Man kann nicht
an das Licht denken
und gleichzeitig an den Tod
an die dampfende Teetasse
und an die Struktur der Trinität
an die Zahnarztrechnung
und an den ersten Kuß
an den Tumor
und an die Windungen der Loire –

Man kann nicht am Denken verzweifeln
und gleichzeitig
denken

SAGE
für Anton

Einer sah
wie der Wind
Lotosblüten
durchs Gras
rollte

und erfand
das Rad

Sehr viel
später erst
erkannte er

daß er nun
neu erfinden mußte:

I

ONE CAN'T

One can't
think of light
and simultaneously of Death
of the steaming tea-cup
the structure of the Trinity
the dentist's bill
and of one's first kiss
of a tumour
and the meandering Loire –

One can't despair about thinking
and simultaneously
think

LEGEND
for Anton

One man saw
how the wind
rolled
lotus-blossoms
through grass

and invented
the wheel

He only
recognised
very much later

he'd have to get down
to inventing again:

Lotosblüten
vom Wind
durchs Gras
gerollt

IMMER WIEDER...

Immer wieder
ist da der
Apfel und
die Hand die
sich ausstreckt

ist da der
Blick
der Biß
die nackte
Erkenntnis

Immer wieder
werden wir
vertrieben
aus einem Garten
den es nie
gegeben hat

SICH ORIENTIEREN

Die Bilder und
die Bilder der Bilder:

Orientierung
für einige Schritte –
doch in welchem Raum?

lotus-blossoms
rolled
by the wind
through grass

AGAIN AND AGAIN...

Again and again
there's the
apple the
hand that keeps
reaching out

there's the
look
the bite
the naked
knowledge

Again and again
we're
expelled
from a garden
that never
existed

FINDING ONE'S BEARINGS

Images and
images of images:

Bearings for
a few steps –
in what dimension though?

Die alten Kartographen
wußten es:
ohne die Ungeheuer
am äußersten Rand
die alles zu
verschlingen drohen
ist jede Karte
unvollständig

MIT EINER TÜTE OBST IM REGEN

Plötzlich
von warmen Tropfen
durchweicht

wird das Packpapier
unter meinen Händen
glatte nackte
Menschenhaut

spüre ich
die Formen der
Früchte –

erschreckt
von soviel unerwarteter
Zärtlichkeit

IN EINEM HOTELZIMMER

Poesie
ist Irrtum –

The ancient cartographers
knew:
without those monsters
on the extreme rim
threatening to
swallow up everything
each map is
incomplete

WITH A BAG OF FRUIT IN THE RAIN

Suddenly
sodden
with tepid drops

the paper turns
in my hands
into smooth sheer
human skin

I can feel
the bony shape
of each fruit –

shocked
at so much unexpected
tenderness

IN A HOTEL ROOM

Poetry
is error –

eine Hand die
schlaftrunken
auf dem Kopfkissen tastet
nach einer
anderen Hand –

und zwischen beiden
liegt der
Atlantik

UNSCHULD DES STEINES

Auch im Stein
fließt eine Quelle
schläft ein Baum
pulsiert die Möglichkeit des Lebens
lauert schon der Gedanke
der Steine zurechtschlägt
Quellen aufspürt
Bäume entwurzelt
das Leben zur
Unmöglichkeit macht

ARISTOTELES HIELT...

Aristoteles hielt
Versteinerungen für
Fehler der Natur
tierische pflanzliche
Formen die (durch welches
Mißlingen?)
in Stein erwacht sind –

a hand which
full of sleep
searches the pillow
for some
other hand –

and in between them
lies the
Atlantic

THE INNOCENCE OF STONE

In stone too
a source is flowing
a tree is sleeping
the possibility of life throbs
already the thought is lurking
which knocks stones into shape
which seeks out sources
uproots trees
makes life
impossible to live

ARISTOTLE THOUGHT...

Aristotle thought
fossils an
error of nature
animal plant
forms which (thanks to
what failure)
have awoken in stone –

Und wir:
wie sind wir
in diesen Granit gekommen
wer hat uns hier
eingepflanzt
und mit welcher
Hoffnung?

STUCK

Was da entsteht
Weiß aus Weiß
was da hervorwächst
aus Kirchendecken Klostermauern
Akanthusranken Muscheln Blüten
und Engelsgesichter
Geheimrezepte in langen
Wintern ersonnen
Leimwasser Bier Eibischwurzel
Tierborsten und geronnene Milch
in den Gips gerührt
was da entsteht
im Liegen bei Zugluft
Husten Gliederreißen Wassersucht
was da hervorwächst
Weiß aus Weiß
und wie es beginnt
nachts schlaflos durchgeschwitzt
zwischen Alptraum
und Morgengrauen
wie es hervortritt
aus der Decke
Posaunen aus Licht
im Finstern

And we:
how did we get
into this granite
who planted us
here
and with what hopes
in mind?

STUCCO

What's coming into being there
light from light
what's growing forth
out of church-ceilings monastery-walls
acanthus tendrils sea-shells blossoms
and angels' faces
secret recipes concocted
over long winters
lime water beer hibiscus root
animal bristles and curdled milk
stirred into the plaster
what's coming into being there
lying down in draughts
coughs rheumatism dropsy
what's growing forth
light from light
and how it begins
at night sleepless covered in sweat
in between nightmares
and dawn's dank fingers
the way it appears
from out of the ceiling
trumpets of light
in the midst of darkness

WIEDERHOLUNGEN

Im Augenblick des Berührens
hast du es schon verfehlt –

darum immer neu
der Vers
die Umarmung
die anrollende
gischtende
Welle

VOM SEHEN

Ich sehe den Korbstuhl
Ich sehe die Kaffeetasse
in der du rührst
Ich sehe – sehr deutlich –
das Gesicht des Kellners

Aber dich?

Jetzt: nur die Haarspitze
die dein Kinn streift
Jetzt: nur dein
Ohrring
der schaukelt
im Licht

NADA

Wie sang – und
klanglos
unser deutsches
„Nichts" –

REPETITIONS

The moment you touch it
you've already missed it –

thus ever new
the verse
the embrace
the wave
which rolls in
shedding its
foam

ON VISION

I see the wickerwork chair
I see the coffee-cup
in which you are stirring
I see – very clearly –
the waiter's face

But what about you?

Now: just the end of a hair
that is touching your chin
Now: just your
earring
that is dangling
in the light

NADA

How little
pomp
and circumstance
in the German word "Nichts" –

Form und Inhalt
entsprechen sich
völlig:
ein Wort das sich
auf der Zunge
verflüchtigt
nichts vormacht
höchstens Philosophen
auf Holzwege lockt –

Nimm dagegen
„nada":

lebendige Silbenfolge
klingt wie
Kindergeplapper
ein Mädchenname ein
kurzer Trompetenstoß

ja, flattert lustig
und bunt
zwischen den Lippen –
ein rotes Tuch
vor den Hörnern
des Stiers

DER KACHELOFEN FLÜSTERT MIT DESCARTES

Ich bin
also denke ich

Fühlst du die Wärme?

Ich bin

Meine Gedanken brennen
Sie kriechen durchs Holz

A sober marriage
of form and content:
a word that
evaporates
on your tongue,
kids no one,
at most has philosophers
barking up forest paths
that end abruptly –

Compare
"nada" though:

live syllables,
sounds like
nattering children,
a girl's name, a
spirited blast on a trumpet

fluttering merrily
colourfully
between your lips –
a red rag
in front of the horns
of the bull

THE TILED STOVE WHISPERS WITH DESCARTES

I am
therefore I think

Can you feel the heat?

I am

My thoughts are on fire
They creep through the wood

Sie knistern in den Buchenscheiten
Sie murmeln seufzen
Sie suchen etwas
indem sie zerstören

Meine Gedanken sind
deine Träume
Du kannst sie hören
wie das Knistern in dir

Ich denke dich
also bin ich

Ich zweifle an dir
Ich brenne vor Zweifel
Im Zweifel bin ich
Gedanken sind Asche
Aber ich brenne
Ich bin heißt:
ich brenne

Fühlst du die Wärme?

Ich bin nicht
die Wärme
Ich bin nicht das Flüstern
das Knistern das Prasseln
Täusche dich nicht
Hinter den Flammen
brenne ich

Ich denke dich
wie du mich denkst

Das ist ein anderes Feuer
eins das keine Wärme gibt
ein Feuer ohne Flammen
ohne Gedanken

They crackle in the beech-logs
murmur sob
they're searching for something
by destroying

My thoughts are
your dreams
You can hear them
like the crackling inside you

I think you
therefore I am

I doubt you
I am burning with doubt
In doubt I am
Thoughts are ash
But I am burning
"I am" means
"I am on fire"

Can you feel the heat?

I am not
the heat
not the whispering
crackling, crepitation
Don't be deceived!
Behind the flames
I am on fire

I'm thinking you
as you're thinking me

This is a different fire
one which provides no heat
a fire without flame
without thoughts

Es flüstert nicht
Es sucht nicht

In diesem Feuer schläft
die Gewißheit

DIESER MOMENT...

Dieser Moment
aus Licht
aus möglichem Licht
aus Erwartung von Licht –

dieser Moment den
außer mir
keiner wahrnahm
(nur eine Eidechse
lief über die
brennende Mauer) –

Etwas
wie ein Beweis

schwer zu sagen
wofür

VON DER WAHRHEIT

In diesem Licht
sitzt sie als Eidechse
auf einem warmen Stein
atmend flüchtig
leicht zu verscheuchen –

It doesn't whisper
It doesn't search

In this fire slumbers
Certitude

THIS MOMENT...

This moment
composed of light
of potential light
expectations of light –

this moment which
no one but I
perceived
(only a lizard
was running across the
burning wall) –

Something
like proof

hard to say
what for

ON TRUTH

In this light
it's sitting, a lizard,
on a warm stone
breathing fleeting
easy to scare off –

Und anderswo
reiten für sie die
verurteilten Ketzer
mit spitzen Hüten
auf Eselsrücken
zum Scheiterhaufen

DAS WUNDER

Nicht selten
ist es eine
minimale Störung
die uns aufschreckt
verzaubert –

Unterstellte man Greco
nicht einen Augenfehler?

Verliebte sich Romeo
in Wahrheit nur
weil Julias Stimme
gerade etwas
heiser war?

Ein Riß in der
Erwartung
eine leichte
Enttäuschung genügt:
daß das Wunder
eintreten kann

And elsewhere
the condemned heretics
with their pointed hats
are riding for it
on donkey's backs
to burn at the stake

THE MIRACLE

It is quite often
some minimal
disturbance
which shakes us up
causes rapture –

Didn't they claim El Greco
had something wrong with his eyes?

Didn't Romeo
really only fall
in love because Juliet's voice
just happened to be
somewhat hoarse at the time?

A fissure in our
expectations
a slight
disappointment are enough
to let the miracle
in

II

OVID ÜBERSETZEN – EINE NACHHILFESTUNDE

Diese unsichere
Mädchenstimme neben mir –
erst noch stockend
mit langen Pausen
dann
plötzlich
immer schneller –
alte Verse von
göttlichen Wundern die sich
neues Leben suchen
neue Gestalt –

Greif nicht ein!
Verbessere nichts!

Was heißt schon
Fehler
wenn zwischen den Worten
also in uns
das Wachs
zu schmelzen beginnt!

SÜDLICHES CAFÉ

Nachmittag aus Licht
und alle Wände
Spiegel,
in denen wir uns
beobachten konnten,
wie wir lachten,
uns küßten,
Aranciata tranken…

II

TRANSLATING OVID – A COACHING SESSION

This girl's voice
uncertain at my side –
at first still halting
making long pauses
then
suddenly
faster ever faster –
old verses about
divine miracles
seeking new life
new form –

Don't intervene!
Don't try to improve on it!

What is a
mistake
when between the words –
inside us, I mean –
the wax
starts to melt!

SOUTHERN CAFÉ

An afternoon of sheer light
and all the walls
were mirrors
in which we could
observe ourselves:
the way we laughed,
kissed each other
or drank aranciata...

All das
veränderte sich
mit einer Bewegung,
als dieser alte Mann
aus dem Dorf
eintrat, die Mütze abnahm
und wir in seinem Nacken
das faustgroße Geschwür
sahen, das plötzlich
aus allen Spiegeln
auftauchte

wohin wir auch
die Köpfe wandten

CASA DI GIULIETTA

Eine Schar Touristen
die sich nicht einigen können
wer zuerst fotografiert wird
vor dem Haus auf dem Balkon
neben der Statue

Die junge Führerin
spielt hilflos mit
ihrem Armband
sieht nur daß es
wieder später wird
schickt ihrem Freund
übers Handy
tausend Küsse

All that
changed
with a single movement
when the old man
from the village
came in, took off his beret
revealing on his neck
the fist-sized swelling
which suddenly
surged up
out of all the mirrors

whichever way we turned
our heads

CASA DI GIULIETTA

A flock of tourists
that can't agree
which of them should be photographed first
in front of the house on the balcony
beside the statue

The young guide
toys helplessly with
her bracelet
only sees she again won't
be getting home on time
uses her cell-phone
to send her boyfriend
a thousand kisses

CASA DI DESDEMONA

Ja, das Haus gibt es wirklich
sagt der Reiseführer
auch wenn unter dem
Spitzbogenfenster wohl nie
eine Desdemona gelehnt hat
der Mord könnte geschehen sein
auch wenn der Mann
kein Mohr war nur Moro hieß
Mißverständnis eines
William Shakespeare der
vermutlich nicht Shakespeare war –

aber das Haus steht
zweifellos da
aus Steinen aus Worten
aus Möglichkeit Irrtum –

jetzt bewegt sich etwas
hinter den Fenstern

SÜDLICHE SZENE

Im Hof zwei
Fünfzehnjährige
werfen einander
ein offenes
Messer zu
immer schneller
immer gefährlicher –

Ein Mädchen lehnt
lächelnd daneben –

Der ganze Abend
ist nur dies
Messerblitzen
der gespannte
Blick

CASA DI DESDEMONA

Yes, the house really exists,
the guide says,
although no Desdemona
presumably ever leant
at the pointed-arch window
the murder could have occurred
although the man
was not a moor but just called Moro
the misunderstanding of some
William Shakespeare who
probably wasn't Shakespeare –

but the house is
undoubtedly standing there,
built of stones, words,
contingency, error –

something's now stirring
behind the windows

SOUTHERN SCENE

In the courtyard two
fifteen-year-olds
are throwing each other
an open
knife
ever faster
ever more dangerous –

A girl is leaning
smiling beside them –

The whole of the evening's
just this
flashing knife
this flushed
look

ENDPUNKT

Eine Bar ohne
Gäste in
der Mittagsstille
Vitrinen voll von
staubigen Pralinen-
schachteln
Torten aus Gips
und leeren Cola-Büchsen
Der Kellner ist
nicht zu finden
An der Wand
das Foto einer
nackten Frau
die seit Jahrzehnten schon
tot ist

MARKT, ABEND

Ein Tag wie jeder
Nichts geschah

Die Obstverkäuferin
gähnend
sucht die zerquetschten
Pfirsiche aus dem Kasten

Beim Fischhändler
der gut verkauft hat
zerschmilzt das Eis
rosig
von Blut

TERMINUS

A bar without
patrons in
noon-day silence
glass-cases full of
dusty chocolate-
boxes
plaster tarts
and empty cola-cans
The waiter is
waiting nowhere at all
On the wall
the photo of a
naked woman
who for decades
has already been dead

MARKET, EVENING

A day like any other
Nothing's happened

Yawning
the woman selling fruit
plucks squashed peaches
out of her crate

At the fishmonger's
where sales have been good
the ice is melting
rosy
with blood

49

OPERNDONNER

Stumpfe Lanzen
Schlingen ohne Knoten

Todesschreie
in Dur und Moll

Das Grauen
vorauszulesen
auf Seite 23 der Partitur –

Daß einmal
im letzten Akt die Carmen
tatsächlich vom Theaterdolch
verletzt
ihr Arie blutend
auf den Kollegen gestützt
zu Ende sang
merkte keiner

LADY MACBETH ALS KLEINES MÄDCHEN

Sie liegt oft nachts
mit offenen Augen und lauscht
in die Dunkelheit
sie hält die Hand über eine
Kerzenflamme
um ihren Willen zu erproben
Sie findet einen Turmfalken
mit gebrochenem Flügel
und pflegt ihn gesund
Sie spielt mit dem Wind
Orakel – treibt er das Blatt
nach links
will sie verdammt sein
Sie verkleidet sich
vor dem Spiegel als Heilige

OPERATIC THUNDER

Blunt lances
nooses without knots

Screams of death
with flats and sharps

The gruesome truth
to be read in advance
if you flick to page 23 of the score –

That once
in the last act Carmen
genuinely injured
by the theatre dagger
completed her aria
leaning bleeding
on her colleague:
nobody noticed

LADY MACBETH AS A LITTLE GIRL

She often lies there at night
open-eyed and listens
her way into the darkness
She holds her hand over a
candle-flame
to test her willpower
She finds a kestrel
whose wing is broken
and nurses it
She plays the oracle game
with the wind – if it wafts
the leaf to the left
it is her will to be damned
She dresses up
in front of the mirror as a saint

Sie wünscht sich einen Dolch
und versteckt die keimenden Brüste
Als sie einmal einen
Gehängten sieht
begreift sie daß der Tod
ein Hampelmann ist
Der Freundin die ihr
geheimes Versteck verrät
gibt sie Tollkirschen zu essen
aber nichts geschieht
Sie weiß als Einzige
daß Wolken
keine Gesichter haben

SCHNAPPSCHUSS, KINDHEIT

Der letzte Sommer
der ihnen blieb –

Noch gut erinnert er sich
an den Badesee:
wie die Mutter mit ihm lachte
weil sie so schief
im Wasser hing
mit nur einem
Lungen
flügel

VORFAHREN

Drei, vier Generationen
überschau ich:
die übrigen
vom Erdboden verschluckt

She wishes for a dagger
and hides her burgeoning breasts
When she comes across
a hanged man
she sees that Death
is a spineless puppet
She gives the girlfriend
who lets on about her secret hideout
deadly nightshade
but nothing happens
She is the only one to know
that clouds
have no faces

SNAPSHOT, CHILDHOOD

The final summer
remaining to them –

He well remembers
that lakeside resort:
the way his mother laughed with him
because she was hanging there
so awry in the water
with only one
lung
lobe

FOREBEARS

Three or four generations
are still within eye-shot:
the earth
has opened and swallowed up

als hätte es sie
nie gegeben –

Nur manchmal
im Aufzucken einer
Anekdote erhellt
seh ich einen von ihnen:

den Offizier etwa
dem laut Familienlegende
ein Kugelblitz
sämtliche Knöpfe
von der Uniform riß –

da steht er
im Dunkeln
in weiter Ferne
ein Zinnsoldat

reglos
starrt zu mir her
als warte er auf
eine Erklärung

FRAGMENT, HISTORISCH

Die Hand meines Urgroßvaters
die Künstlerhand   .
die Malerhand
um 1900
in Gips abgegossen
von einem Freund –

(Meine Mutter als Kind
verbarg sie nachts
panisch unter ihrer Schürze

the rest as though
they'd never existed –

Only at times
in the flickering light
of an anecdote
do I glimpse one of them:

the officer for instance who,
according to the family legend,
had all the buttons
torn from his uniform
by ball lightning –

there he is standing
in the dark
a long way off
a tin-soldier

motionless
staring across to me
as though he were waiting for
an explanation

HISTORICAL FRAGMENT

My great-grandfather's hand
this artist's hand
painter's hand
cast in plaster
by a friend
around 1900 –

(As a child my mother
hid it in panic
at night beneath her pinafore

um nicht denken zu müssen
an die abgerissenen
Gliedmaßen
der Luftangriffe –)

Die Hand meines Urgroßvaters
liegt auf meinem Schreibtisch

seltsamer Findling
unnahbares Objekt
amputierte Berührung –

und greift doch
nach mir

wird Jahr um Jahr
ähnlicher
meiner Hand

LEIDENSSTÄTTE

Kein fensterloses
Verlies und keine
ausgefeilten
Folterwerkzeuge:
nur ein leeres
Zimmer einige
alltägliche Gegenstände –

die Hölle
wie der Himmel
kommt aus
mit fast nichts

so as not to have to think
of the torn-off
limbs
left by the air-raids –)

My great-grandfather's hand
is here on my writing-table

outlandish foundling
unapproachable object
amputated touch –

and yet it is clutching
at me

with every passing year
becomes more similar
to my hand

PLACE OF SUFFERING

No windowless
dungeon no
polished
instruments of torture:
just an empty
room and a scatter
of everyday things –

hell
like heaven
can make do
with almost nothing

III

GEDICHTE

Jene Art
der Erkenntnis
die auf Täuschung
beruht

einer Luftdruck-
schwankung

dem plötzlich
veränderten Licht

die leicht
widerlegbar scheint
auf den zweiten Blick

auf den ersten aber
verstummen läßt

BLICK ZWISCHEN ZWEI SPIEGEL

Dieses Gedicht
schreibe ich von
Vivaldi ab –

Vivaldi wiederum
hat seine Töne
nach dem Fall
einiger Herbstblätter
gesetzt –

Wen ahmten die
Blätter nach?

III

POEMS

That kind
of perception
that's based
on deception

on a fluctuation
in atmospheric pressure

on a sudden change
in the light

a kind which seems
easy to refute
at second glance

but which, first time round,
makes you mute

GLANCE BETWEEN TWO MIRRORS

This poem
I'm plagiarising
from Vivaldi –

Vivaldi in turn
strung together his notes
to mime the way some autumn leaves
had fallen –

Whom were the
leaves imitating?

VON DER BLINDHEIT

Lange sprechen wir
über den Baum mit
Bitterorangen
betasten die Früchte
wiegen sie
in der Hand –

Später über dem Meer
überreif
rötlich von Saharastaub
der Mond –

Wie werd ich es los
das Metaphernfieber?

ORTE

Zum Beispiel
Linzer Gasse 7
Engel-Apotheke
wo für Trakl
der Totentanz
mit dem Kokain begann –

Ich werde mich nur
an das junge Mädchen
auf dem Fahrrad
erinnern das dort
im Platzregen
laut singend
an mir vorbeischoß

ON BLINDNESS

For a long time we talk
about the tree with
the bitter oranges
We feel its fruit
weigh it
in our hands –

Later above the sea
overripe
and reddish with dust from the Sahara
sways the moon –

How can I shake off
this metaphor-fever?

PLACES

Take for example
"Angel's", the chemists,
in that lane
(7 Linzer Gasse)
where for Trakl
the dance of death
with cocaine began –

I'll only be able to recall
the young girl
on the bicycle
who shot past me there
in the heavy downpour
singing at the top of her voice

BIOGRAFIEN

Der Dichter starb

weil er im Eis
einbrach

weil er beim Füttern
der Tauben
aus dem Fenster stürzte

weil ihn ein Ast
erschlug
auf den Champs-Elysées

weil er das Hölzchen
der Olive in
seinem Martini verschluckte –

es mangelt nie
an plausiblen Gründen

IM INNEREN DER BÜCHER...

Im Inneren der Bücher
ist es still –

Kein Nachhall
vom Gezänk der Hauswirtin
des Dichters
vom Kanonendonner vor Jena –

Im Inneren auch der
schreiendsten Worte
ist es still –

Als wären sie angekommen
wohin wir vielleicht nie
gelangen können –

BIOGRAPHIES

The poet died

because the ice
broke

because he plummeted
down from the window
while feeding the pigeons

because a branch
came down on him
on the Champs-Elysées

because he choked on
the stick through the olive
in his martini –

there's never a lack
of plausible motives

INSIDE THE BOOKS...

Inside the books
is quietude –

No echo
of the poet's landlady's
nagging
the rumble of guns outside Jena -

Inside the very
loudest of words
is quietude –

As though they'd arrived
at a place which we
may never reach –

Auch wenn du dir
die Ohren verstopfst:
wie von fern her
der Sirenengesang
des Blutes

DEM BILDHAUER JOSEF A. HENSELMANN

Wieder kehren wir
zu den Ursprüngen
zurück:

du in die Marmorbrüche
in denen noch heute
ebenso viele Arbeiter
sterben
wie im Mittelalter

ich in die Sprachbrüche
wo das aufgesprengte
Schweigen uns trifft
mit der ganzen Wucht
seiner allerersten
Splitter

WORTE

Müdigkeit der Worte –
Überdruß der Worte –
Leere der Worte –

Mein Urgroßvater
wußte nichts davon

Even if you
plug your ears:
as though from far away
the siren song
of the blood

TO THE SCULPTOR JOSEF A. HENSELMANN

Back to
the origins
once again:

you to the marble-quarries
in which
as many workers
die today
as in the dark ages

me to the language-quarries
where silence
blasted open with explosive
hits us with the full force
of its very first
splinters

WORDS

The weariness at the heart of words –
The surfeit at the heart of words –
The emptiness at the heart of words –

My grandfather's father
knew nothing of this

Er besaß nur zwei Bücher

Zwischen Pflug und Stall
murmelte er Verse

Eine Zeile konnte ihn
mehr überraschen
als ein Morgen
klirrend
von Rauhreif

MANCHMAL

Als ob die Worte
mehr sehen könnten
als wir

Ihr Fell sträubt sich

Sie wollen nicht gehorchen

Sie knurren die Tür an

Aber draußen
ist niemand

FINIS OPERIS

Tatsächlich: es
gibt sie die Augenblicke
in denen uns
der letzte Pinselstrich
gelingt
der leuchtende Schlußsatz

Had only two books

Murmured verses
between ploughed field and cattle-shed

A line could
surprise him more
than a morning
jangling
with hoar-frost

SOMETIMES

As though words
were able to see more
than we can

Their fur is bristling

They won't obey

They're growling at the door

But there is no one
outside

FINIS OPERIS

They really exist
these moments
when we do
accomplish
the final brush-stroke
the bright dying fall

die Einstellung mit der
der Film
enden müßte –

Aber dann?

Es geht einfach alles weiter:
die Zeit läuft
(ob du willst oder nicht)
bis der Pinsel
Borsten verliert
die Feder das Papier
zerkratzt
und nur noch
Schatten
über die Leinwand flimmern

the take with which
the film
should end –

What then?

Things simply carry on:
time runs its course
(if you like it or not)
until the brush
is shedding bristles
the nib is scratching
holes in the paper
and all
that's flickering
over the screen
are shadows

IV

DIE ALTEN BILDER

Einmal muß das
ganz einfach gewesen sein:
gab es die fraglose
Leidenschaft für die
Gegenstände
wurden Faltenwürfe
Fingerhaltungen
Lichtreflexe auf Waffen
in zahllosen Skizzen
wiederholt
und bis zur
Vollkommenheit
getrieben –

Dann plötzlich
– wann war das –
wandten sich die
Dinge von uns ab
verschwammen uns vor
den Augen lösten sich auf
Farben Formen tanzten
uns entgegen –

Aber noch immer
stehen wir voller Neid
vor dem einfältigen Leben
eines jahrhundertealten
Blumenstraußes

sehen atemlos
die Fleischwerdung
des Göttlichen selbst
in einem Kind auf
leuchtend weißem Linnen
auf fühlbar knisterndem
Stroh

IV

OLD PAINTINGS

Once it must have been
very simple:
there was that unquestioning
passion for objects
the way folds fall
the way fingers clutch things
the way light plays on weapons
were rehearsed
in countless sketches
worked up
to perfection –

Then abruptly
(when exactly?)
objects turned
away from us
blurred in front
of our eyes dissolved
colours forms started dancing
towards us –

Yet still
we stand filled with envy
in front of the artless life
of a bunch of flowers
which is centuries old

breathlessly watch
the incarnation
of the Divine itself
in a child on glowing white linen
on palpably crackling
straw

ADAM UND EVA IN EINER FRÜHEN DARSTELLUNG

Nicht von schöner
Gestalt nicht
Inbegriff der Fruchtbarkeit
und auch ohne
das Lächeln der
Versuchung –

klein sind ihre
schwindsüchtigen Körper
jede Rippe darauf ist
deutlich zu erkennen:
sie mit ausgetrockneten
Brüsten
er zum Jagen zu schwach
ein Sammler von
Beeren
und beide nur
zu wenigen
Verständigungslauten
fähig –

Adam und Eva
wie sie aussahen
Jahrtausende
vor der Erfindung
des Paradieses

RÖMISCHES MOSAIK (EINEN NICHT GEFEGTEN BODEN NACH EINEM GASTMAHL DARSTELLEND)

Merkwürdiges Motiv
merkwürdiger Auftraggeber –

wichtiger als
der Prunk seiner Feste
die exotischen Delikatessen

AN EARLY REPRESENTATION OF ADAM AND EVE

Not fair of
frame no
paragon of fruitfulness
and also devoid
of the smile of
temptation –

their bodies are
consumptive and small
each rib can
clearly be discerned:
she with desiccated
breasts
he too weak for hunting
a collector of
berries
and both only
capable of a few sounds
to make themselves
understood to each other –

Adam and Eve
the way they looked
thousands of years
before the invention
of paradise

ROMAN MOSAIC (SHOWING AN UNSWEPT FLOOR
AFTER A BANQUET)

A singular theme
a singular client –

what mattered more
to him
than the splendour of his feasts

als Gelächter Tanz
und Umarmungen
war ihm
im leeren Saal
auf Überresten
und Abfällen
das immer klarere
Morgenlicht

DORFSTRASSE VAN HET BILT (JAN VAN GOYEN)

Bilder wie dieses:
eine Dorfstraße
an einem schönen Tag
die Leute plaudernd
vor windschiefen
Häusern mit Taubenschlägen
einer schmaucht
seine Pfeife ein
Fuhrwerk steht
mitten im Weg –

glücklich
nennt man Zeiten
die solchen Frieden noch
in solcher Deutlichkeit
wünschen konnten

VERSUCHUNG DES HL. ANTONIUS

Der Heilige
zu Boden gezerrt
von Dämonen
getreten gebissen

exotic dainties
than laughter dance
and lovers in one other's arms
was – in the empty hall
on leftovers
and detritus –
the morning light
growing ever more lucid

VILLAGE STREET VAN HET BILT (JAN VAN GOYEN)

Pictures like this one:
a village street
on a beautiful day
the people chatting
in front of crooked
houses with dovecots
one man is puffing away
at his pipe
a cart's there in the
middle of the path –

happy
the times
which could still
desire such peace
with so much clarity

THE TEMPTATION OF ST. ANTHONY

The saint
pulled down to the ground
by demons
kicked and bitten

an den Haaren geschleift
und dennoch
unbeirrt standhaft –

nicht gezeigt
hat uns Grünewald
die wahre Versuchung:

die völlige Stille
wenn alle Geister
von ihm abgelassen haben
und nichts mehr
zwischen ihm und
der Sünde steht
als ein Gedanke

GALLERIA PITTI, FLORENZ

Im schlendernden Schritt
von Bild zu Bild

Blicke wie in Sommerabendfenster –

Warum wächst die Stille
in mir
auch wenn dort der heftigste
Aufruhr tobt?

Lange betrachte ich den
gischtenden Faltenwurf
die dunklen Augen
der Judith –

Allori heißt es habe in ihr
seine Geliebte porträtiert

dragged by the hair
still stands his ground
unswervingly –

Grünewald has declined
to show us
the true temptation:

the desert of silence
when all the spirits
have left him alone
and all that
separates him
from sin
is a single thought

GALLERIA PITTI, FLORENCE

Ambling along
from painting to painting

Glancing as though into windows on summer evenings –

Why does the silence inside me
grow
though the most violent tumult
is raging out there?

I gaze for a long while
at Judith
the foaming folds on her dress
her sombre eyes –

Allori, it's said, portrayed
in her his mistress

im abgeschlagenen
Haupt des Holofernes
das sie an den Haaren
hochhebt
sich selbst

PIERO DELLA FRANCESCA MALT DIE SCHLACHT
AN DER MILVISCHEN BRÜCKE

Die Schlacht – sie ist vorbei – sie brennt noch immer.
Doch nur so kalt wie dieser kalte Schimmer
Auf Rüstungen. Der Lanzenwald steht starr.
Der Tod, den man hier stirbt – er ist nicht schlimmer
Als wenn die Wolke dort im Blau zerfließt...
Die Perspektiven zieht ein Lautenstimmer,
Der bis ins Lautlose die Saiten spannt.
Kein Pferdebrüllen, Stöhnen. Kein Gewimmer.
Kein Blut spritzt grell, trieft von der Freskowand.
Das Schlachtfeld – wie ein aufgeräumtes Zimmer.

ANSICHT EINER IDEALEN STADT
aus der Schule von Piero della Francesca

Als wärst du unter diesen
Arkaden schon
einmal gegangen –

Der Rundbau mit den Säulenreihen
die ausgebleichten Palazzi
wie Zitate

Ganz natürlich
wuchert staubiges Grün
über die Balkone

in the severed
head of Holofernes
that she's holding up
by the hair
himself

PIERO DELLA FRANCESCA PAINTS THE BATTLE
AT THE MILVIC BRIDGE

The battle's over – it is still aflame.
But only as coldly as this frigid gleam
On armour. Forests of lances stand and bristle.
The death you die here feels no more like doom
Than when that cloud dissolves into the azure…
A lute-tuner's driving the perspectives home,
Tightening the strings until there is no sound.
No bellowing horse, no moans you could exhume.
No blood spurts gaudily, drips from the frescoed wall.
The battlefield – a neatly cleared-up room.

VIEW OF AN IDEAL CITY
from the school of Piero della Francesca

As though you'd already
passed beneath
these archways before –

The rotunda with its rows of columns
the faded palazzi
like quotations

Quite naturally
dusty green runs riot
across the balconies

Am Himmel
ein paar Wolkenfetzen

Hinter der angelehnten Tür
erwartet dich
Schattengeruch

Aber die Menschen fehlen

Diese Stille auf
den ersonnenen Straßen

Diese Stille wie
nach einem
Pogrom

DIE UNS ANSEHEN

In den Bildern
gibt es Bilder –

In den Bildern
gibt es Spiegel –

In den Bildern
gibt es angelehnte Türen –

In den Bildern
gibt es Fenster
durch die Licht fällt –

In den Bildern
gib es Augen
die uns ansehen
als käme das Licht
von uns

In the sky
a few wisps of cloud

Behind that door left ajar
the smell of shadows
awaits you

But there are no people

What peace in
these invented streets

The peace which settles
after a
pogrom

WHICH ARE LOOKING AT US

Within the pictures
there are pictures –

Within the pictures
there are mirrors –

Within the pictures
there are doors standing slightly open –

Within the pictures
there are windows
light's falling through –

Within the pictures
there are eyes
which are looking at us
as though we were
the source of the
light

ENTFERNUNGEN

Ich stelle die Uhr zurück
gegen die Müdigkeit
rechne nach vorn
was du gerade tust
ob du wach bist schläfst
wie weit ich entfernt bin
von dir von mir
zwischen jaulenden
Polizeiautos Taxis
wie endlos unterwegs
unter den Türmen
der Fifth Avenue
wie weit entfernt von mir
und plötzlich
angekommen
vor La Tours Büßerin
die reglos sitzt
in der rasenden Stadt
nur die Kerze sieht
die Flamme:
sie brennt so hell
so furchtlos
vor dem dunklen
Spiegel

BERNINIS DAPHNE

Jede Berührung
ist Verwandlung

berührt nicht was
sie berühren will
berührt im Verfehlen
berührt was
in der Berührung
erst wächst –

82

DISTANCES

I put back my watch
to combat the tiredness
and think ahead
to what you're now doing
whether you're awake or sleeping
how far I'm removed
from you from me
between these proverbially howling
police-cars taxis for ever
in transit
beneath the towers
on Fifth Avenue
how far removed from myself
and suddenly
in my own skin
in front of La Tour's Penitent Woman
who's sitting motionless
in this breakneck city
who only sees the candle
sees the flame:
it's burning so bright
so fearless
in front of the sombre
mirror

BERNINI'S DAPHNE

Every touch
is a transformation

doesn't touch what
it's out to touch
touches while missing
touches what
only grows
during touching –

unter tastenden
Fingern entstehen
Rinde
Blätter
Menschenhaut
atmender
Stein

VERMEER

Wie schwer, die stille Welt zu konstruieren.
Der Tisch – er steht nicht ruhig. Es pulsieren
Der Krug, das Tuch, die Karte an der Wand.
Die goldnen Nägel in dem Stuhl vibrieren –
Sie halten ihn mit Mühe nur am Platz.
Was für ein Licht! Ein Tosen, Explodieren,
In dem die Bleiglasscheibe fast zerspringt!
Und doch: die junge Frau beim Musizieren
Dreht sich nicht um. Die Spitzenklöpplerin
Hebt nicht den Blick – sie muß sich konzentrieren,
Daß ihr kein Faden durcheinander kommt.
Wie leicht die Dinge den Verstand verlieren!

TOD DES MALERS

Ein weißes Pferd
sich aufbäumend
gesattelt doch
ohne Reiter –

Eins der letzten Bilder
die man in der Werkstatt
später finden wird

beneath fumbling
fingers
bark
leaves
human skin
breathing stone
come into being

VERMEER

The silent world – how hard to recreate.
The table – won't stand still. They all pulsate:
The jug, the cloth, the map up on the wall.
The golden nails sunk in the chair vibrate –
Can only just about keep it in place.
What light! Its particles stream and detonate,
Causing the leaded glass to almost crack!
And yet the girl whose melodies sound sweet
Doesn't turn round. The woman making lace
Doesn't look up. She's got to concentrate
To make sure that her threads don't get confused.
How things freak out and start to resonate!

DEATH OF THE PAINTER

A white horse
rearing up
saddled but
without a rider –

One of the last paintings
that they'll find
in his studio later

Abschiede
für die Überlieferung

Die stürzende Perspektive
kopfüber
zwischen den Fieberkissen

die Fliege die
wieder und wieder
gegen das Wasserglas prallt

bleiben uns
erspart

JUNGE FRAU, NACH RENOIR

Der Regen ist vorbei. Die Schirme stehen
Noch dicht gedrängt im Glanz. Nur aus Versehen
Streift dich ein Blick aus ihren dunklen Augen.
Es freut sie, in der weichen Luft zu gehen.
Mag sein, sie hat gerade noch geweint.
Sie ist dabei, den Freund zu hintergehen.
Sie muß heut abend noch ein Täubchen schlachten.
Was wird sie von der Jungfrau wohl erflehen?
Schlägt unbemerkt ein zweites Herz in ihr?
Zerreißt ihr Lächeln bald schon unter Wehen?
Wie weich die Luft jetzt ist! Wie schön zu gehen!
Ein Blick. Du wirst sie niemals wiedersehen.

GRASHÜPFER

Kann man so etwas
heute noch
erschaffen?

Leave-takings
swelling the great tradition

The plunging perspective
head-first
between the feverish pillows

the fly which
again and again
keeps bumping into the tumbler:

these
we are spared

YOUNG WOMAN, AFTER RENOIR

The rain has stopped. Umbrellas are still here,
Standing and jostling in the light. Her pair
Of dark eyes brushes you by accident.
She's glad to walk out in such languorous air.
It's possible she may have just been crying.
She's out to cheat on her boyfriend. Does she care?
Before tonight's out she must kill a pigeon.
What is she going to ask the virgin for?
Has she a second heart beating inside?
Will labour start soon, causing her smile to tear?
What languorous air! How good to be out walking!
One glance. You'll never see her any more.

GRASSHOPPER

Could one create
such a thing
these days?

Dieses altmodische
Elfengrün
Mittsommernachtstraum-
romantik
bis in die langen Fühler
mit altmeisterlichem
Pinsel gezeichnet –

ein Wesen das
beim besten Willen
nicht zur
Halogenlampe paßt
auf der es sitzt –

Aber jemand
der ein anderes
Kunstideal hat
als wir
macht unbeirrt
weiter

This out-of-date
elfin green,
midsummer night's dream
romance
right up to its beetling feelers,
drawn by a past master's
brush –

a creature which
with the best will in the world
doesn't fit
the halogen lamp
that it's alighted on –

But someone
whose concept of art's
unlike ours
is keeping
unswervingly
at it

V

SEKUNDE

Nichts wiederholt sich
Es gibt nur diesen
einen Augenblick
dieses eine Gesicht
erhellt von Erwartung
und zu großer Ungeduld um
Licht zu machen
dieses eine Augenpaar
das im Glimmen der Holzkohle
den Liebesbrief
überfliegt –

Vor tausend Jahren
eben jetzt
notiert es Sei Shonagon
in ihr
Kopfkissenbuch

ZU EINEM FOTO DER FRANZISKA ZU REVENTLOW

Die verführerischen Augen
einer Toten
Augen die wissen daß
die Augen von Toten
nicht mehr verführen –

(Niemand verläßt für sie
Frau und Kind
Niemand schießt sich
für sie eine
Kugel ins Herz)

V

SECOND

Nothing repeats itself
There's only this
one moment this
one face
illuminated by expectation
and too great impatience to
make light
this one pair of eyes
that skims across
the love-letter
in the charcoal glimmer –

A thousand years ago
this moment
Sei Shonagon is noting it down
in her
pillow book

ON A PHOTO OF FRANZISKA ZU REVENTLOW

Seductive eyes
of a woman who's dead
eyes that know that
dead people's eyes
no longer seduce –

(Nobody leaves
wife and children for them
Nobody goes and
shoots themselves in the heart
for their sake)

Diese Augen
ohne den Schimmer
eines Versprechens
ohne das leiseste
Flackern der
Möglichkeit

sehen mich an

bis ich es bin
der wegsieht

BRIEF

Dieser Sommer der
nur aus deiner
Abwesenheit bestand –

Ich fühlte dich überall
selbst im Fell
einer verwilderten Katze
selbst im Luftzug aus
dem Metro-Schacht

All diese Zärtlichkeiten
zwischen uns –

ich werde sie dir
nie erklären können

IDEE

Im völlig dunklen Zimmer
das Rascheln deines Kleides das
zu Boden fällt

These eyes
without even the gleam
of a promise
the slightest
flicker of
potential

are looking at me

until it is I
who look away

LETTER

This summer which
only consisted of your
absence –

I felt you everywhere
even in the fur
of a cat that had strayed far from home
even in the draught coming from
the metro shaft

All those endearments,
embraces between us –

I'll never be able
to make you feel them

IDEA

In the entirely dark room
the rustling of your dress as it
falls to the floor

URBILD

Am Ende dieses
zerrissenen Tages
sitzt du allein
am Tisch
zeichnest für mich
dein Gesicht:
so
wie du immer
aussehen
wolltest

SCHWARZE NACHT

Wie fern du
mir bist

In deinem Nacken
ein einzelnes Haar
zittert
unter meinem
Atem

FRESKO, VIELFACH ÜBERMALT

Im Regenglanz
Vor der überfüllten Metro
Am verschneiten Ufer
Auf Krankenhausgängen
In frostigen Parks
Zwischen flirrenden Bäumen
lachend verzweifelt erregt:
deine Augen deine Halslinie
dein Haar –

ORIGINAL BENEATH ALL THE COPIES

At the end of this
tattered day
you sit alone
at the table
draw for me
your face:
the way
you always
wanted
to look

BLACK NIGHT

How far you are
from me

On your neck
a single hair is
quivering
in the storm of my
breath

FRESCO, REPEATEDLY PAINTED OVER

In the lustre of the rain
In front of the overcrowded metro
On the snow-covered shore
In hospital corridors
In frost-bound parks
Between blurry trees
laughing desperate excited:
your eyes the line of your neck
your hair –

Jeder Pinselstrich
ein Neubeginn
eine Zerstörung

VON DER TREUE
"Gedanken sind nicht Taten"
Shakespeare, *Maß für Maß*

Erkläre den Gang der
Komödie –

Angelo also schlief
mit Mariane im Glauben sie sei
Isabella

Also betrog er sie –
doch mit wem?

Nicht mit Isabella
denn sie wartete vor der Tür
Nicht mit Isabellas Körper
denn er berührte sie nicht
Nicht mit der Vorstellung ihres Körpers
denn er hatte ihn nie gekannt
Nicht mit einem Gedanken
denn er tastete im Dunkeln
wirkliche warme Glieder –

Also schlief er mit Mariane die
nicht Mariane sein wollte
Also schlief er mit
der Zärtlichkeit Marianes
die Isabella heißen konnte
Also schlief er mit dem
Körper Marianes der die Vorstellung
von Isabellas Körper sein konnte

Each brush-stroke
a new beginning
an act of destruction

ON FIDELITY

"Thoughts are no subjects; intents but merely thoughts"
Shakespeare, *Measure for
Measure*

Explain how the comedy
plays out –

Angelo thus slept
with Mariana believing she was
Isabella

Thus he deceived her –
but with whom?

Not with Isabella
for she was waiting outside the door
Not with Isabella's body
for he did not touch it
Not with the idea of her body
for he had never got to know it
Not with a thought
for his hands felt
real warm limbs in the dark –

Thus he slept with Mariana who
didn't want to be Mariana
Thus he slept with
Mariana's tenderness
which may have been called Isabella
Thus he slept with Mariana's
body which may have been the idea
of Isabella's

also schlief er mit dem Wissen Marianes
daß er sie nur für Isabella hielt
Also schlief er mit der Mariane
die er seit jeher in Mariane
und Isabella gesucht hatte
Also schlief er mit Mariane
die als Isabella auch
an Mariane erinnerte
Also schlief er mit Mariane
die verzweifelt Mariane
sein wollte

Also schlief er mit Mariane
und nur mit ihr

Diese Illusion ist so gut
wie jede andere

VON DER TEILNAHMSLOSEN WELT

Am Ende immer
wie bei Flaubert:

Die verhängten Droschkenfenster
das Paar im Dunklen
das sich auflöst
und findet
in stummen Ekstasen –

und draußen
grelles Mittagslicht
gleichgültige Straßen
Plätze Alleen
reglos unter den
dröhnenden Hufen
das mächtige

Thus he slept with Mariana's knowledge
he only considered her to be Isabella
Thus he slept with the Mariana
whom he had always been searching for
in Mariana and Isabella
Thus he slept with Mariana
who as Isabella as well
reminded him of Mariana
Thus he slept with Mariana
who desperately wished
to be Mariana

Thus he slept with Mariana
and only with her

This illusion is as good
as any other

ON THE UNCONCERNED WORLD

It's always in the end
like in Flaubert:

the draped cab-windows
the couple there in the dark
dissolving
and finding itself
in mute ecstasies –

and outside
the strident light of noon
indifferent streets
squares avenues
immobile beneath the
rumbling hooves
the mighty

allesverschlingende
Gähnen
des Kutschers

all-engulfing
yawn
of the coachman

VI

HÖHLENBILDER

Pferde aus dem Dunkel
hervorbrechend
archaisch ihre langgezogenen
Körper auf denen keiner
reiten wird ihre schmalen Köpfe
die das Nichts
nicht erschreckt

Was wir Geist nennen
diese unbegreifliche
gläserne Kugel in uns
Schwachstelle der Evolution
zersplittert tonlos
unter dem scharfen Rhythmus
ihrer Hufe

PALÄONTOLOGISCHES MUSEUM

All diese Klauen Kiefer
Reißzähne
um Beute zu machen –

All diese Nackenschilde
Stachelpanzer Sprunggelenke
um nicht Beute zu werden –

Jetzt wandert das
gleichgültige Winterlicht
über die Skelette
von Säbelzahntiger
Triceratops
und Pteranodon

VI

CAVE PAINTINGS

Horses bounding
out of the darkness
archaic their elongated
bodies on which no man
will ride narrow heads
that Nothingness
does not dismay –

What we call mind
that incomprehensible
glass-ball inside us
the weakest link of evolution
splinters to pieces without a sound
beneath the harsh rhythm
of their hooves

PALAEONTOLOGICAL MUSEUM

All these claws these jaws
these fangs
to generate prey –

All these neck-guards
barbed armour ankle-joints
so as not to end up as prey –

Winter's indifferent light
is now prowling
across skeletons
of sabre-toothed tigers
triceratops
and pteranodon

das gleichgültige Licht
in dem ich sitze
für ein paar Augenblicke
als rastendes
Tier

HOMO SAPIENS

Der auf Knien der
mit einer Zahnbürste
das Pflaster scheuern muß –

Die in den Schaftstiefeln
ihr dröhnendes Gelächter –

Der Philosoph der lehrt
der Mensch sei das
Tier
das lachen kann

VOM GEIST

Natürlich ist es
die Kehle des
Feindes zu suchen
natürlich
das Mark aus seinen
Knochen zu saugen –

was für ein Wahnsinn dagegen
Worte zu notieren
das Licht in gotischen
Rosetten zu betrachten
an einem Regennachmittag

the same indifferent light
I sit in
for a few moments
a beast
at rest

HOMO SAPIENS

The man down on his knees who's fated
to scrub the cobblestones
with a toothbrush –

The men in jack-boots
their booming guffaws –

The philosopher who teaches
that man is the
animal
gifted with laughter

A DISQUISITION ON THE HUMAN SPIRIT

It's only human nature
to search for
your enemy's throat
It's only human nature
to suck the marrow
out of his juicy bones –

what madness by contrast
to note down words
to contemplate the light
indwelling Gothic rosettes
or on a rainy afternoon

in einer fremden Stadt
die aussichtslose
Liebe zu erfinden

DIE ALLTÄGLICHEN...

Die alltäglichen
Worte alltäglichen Dinge –

Wie sehr wir uns
anklammern an ihren
trügerischen
Schutz –

Heute sah ich
das Bild eines Mannes
der lief durch
Granatenhagel
wie durch Sommerregen:
mit einer über
den Kopf gehaltenen
Zeitung

FOTO

Immer wieder
betrachte ich
dieses Paar:
beide
gleichermaßen jung
und erstaunlich
schön –

in an unknown city
to go and invent
a love without an earthly chance

THE COMMONPLACE...

The commonplace
words, the commonplace things –

how much we
cling to
the shelter
they don't give –

Today I saw
a photo of some man
running through
a hail of shell-fire
as through summer rain:
with a newspaper
held up above
his head

PHOTO

Again and again
I look at
this couple:
both
equally young
and surpassingly
lovely –

wirklich
man könnte
Romeo und Julia
besetzen
mit diesem Soldaten
und dem Mädchen
das aufschreit
unter seinen
Schlagstockhieben

FÜHRUNG

Beachten Sie bitte
dieses Steinschloßgewehr
aus dem 18. Jahrhundert
mit auswechselbaren
Kammern:
eckige Geschosse
galten als wirksamer
gegen Heiden
runde gegen Christen –

ein durch die Aufklärung
freilich
längst überwundener
Unterschied

LAGO DI TOVEL

Hier, sagt man, genau hier der Ort
hier in dieser Gebirgsstille
in Legendenzeit
das Gemetzel

honestly
you could
cast this soldier
as Romeo
the girl
who cries
in the rain
of his blows
as Juliet

GUIDED TOUR

Please take a look at
this flintlock pistol
from the 18th century
with replaceable
chambers:
square shot
was thought to be more efficacious
against the heathens
round shot against the Christians –

a distinction
made redundant
it's true
long ago
by the Enlightenment

LAGO DI TOVEL

Here, they say, here exactly the place
here in this mountain tranquillity
in time out of mind
the butchery,

sagt man ein ganzes Heer
samt seiner Königin
ersäuft erschlagen
das schäumende Wasser
rot von Blut –

noch bis in die
fünfziger Jahre sagt man
verfärbte der See
sich jeden Sommer
(Es gibt Fotos, Signore!) –

Jetzt aber liegt er
kühl und reglos
im nüchternen Licht

Ein Augenzeuge
den nicht kümmert
was du glaubst

WEISHEITEN FÜR GEMÄSSIGTE KLIMAZONEN

Das Scheitern ist eine Lehre
Der Schmerz könnte
Bedeutung haben
Geduld lohnt sich am Ende
Es gibt das Barockkonzert
Es gibt die aufmunternde Stimme
des Arztes
Es gibt die Hand auf deiner Schulter
Kein Kind geht einfach so
verloren

they say, a whole army
along with its queen
drowned clubbed to death
the foaming water
red with blood –

Right up into
the Fifties, they say,
the lake changed
colour every summer
(there are photos, Signore!) –

Now though it's lying
cool, motionless
in the sober light

an eye-witness
unconcerned by what
you happen to believe

WISDOMS FOR MODERATE CLIMATES

Failure's a doctrine like any other
Pain could
have meaning
Patience pays off in the end
There are Baroque concerts
There is the doctor's
encouraging voice
There is the hand resting on your shoulder
No child gets lost
just like that

WAS WUNDERST DU DICH...

Was wunderst du dich
noch immer zu lesen
von RASSE
BLUT und VOLK –

auch bei den
Wörtern
haben primitive Organismen
hat Ungeziefer
die besten
Überlebenschancen

UMSTEIGEN

Dachau, sagt die Stimme
aus dem Lautsprecher
und klingt nach Bauernkaff
und Sommerfrische –

Als hätte hier immer nur
Ludwig Thomas
Lokalbahn verkehrt

Die träge Welt
ist die wahrscheinlichere

Behäbig steigt Rauch
aus einem Kamin

Ein Käfer müht sich
über die erhitzten Gleise
die arglos dösen
bis zum nächsten
Zug

WHY ARE YOU SURPRISED...

Why are you surprised
to still read
of RACE
BLOOD and VOLK –

in the case of
words too
primitive organisms
vermin
have the best
chance of surviving

CHANGING TRAINS

Dachau, the voice
from the loudspeaker says
and it sounds like a rustic hamlet
a spot for summer vacations –

As though some idyllic Bavarian writer's
local railway
had been the only one to run

The lethargic world's
the more plausible one

Snugly smoke's rising
from a chimney

A beetle's struggling
across the hot rails
that are guilelessly dozing
until the next
train comes

VON DER ABSTRAKTION

Ja, die sauberen
Allgemeinbegriffe –

die Frauen links
die Männer rechts

auf einen Haufen
die Mäntel

auf einen Haufen
die Schuhe

auf einen Haufen
die Brillen

auf einen Haufen
das Zahngold

DER SCHMERZ

Härteste aller Währungen
die überall gilt –

Universale Sprache
die keine Übersetzer braucht –

Verläßlicher als
Glück und Freude –

Eindeutiger als die Liebe –

Die eine
immer straff gespannte
Saite in uns
nach der wir
alle anderen Saiten
stimmen können

ON ABSTRACTION

Yes, those neat-and-tidy
general terms –

on the left women
on the right men

in one heap
the coats

in one heap
the shoes

in one heap
the glasses

in one heap
the gold wrenched out
of their teeth

PAIN

Hardest of all currencies
that's legal tender everywhere –

Universal language
in need of no translators –

More reliable than
happiness and joy –

More unequivocal than love –

The one
perpetually taut
string in us
which we can use
to tune
all the others

VII

LUIGI P.

Durch leere Parks, durch Gassen und Alleen
Seh ich ihn in der Abenddämmrung gehen
In Schweigen ganz verhüllt – und Schritt um Schritt
Wird um ihn alles fremd. Was ist geschehen?
Er zögert. Stutzt. Sagt doch: Ist das ein Scherz?
Schon haben alle, die vorübergehen,
Schlohweißes Haar, und manche sind darunter,
Die seinen frühren Freunden ähnlich sehen.
Er fröstelt, zieht den Mantel um sich enger.
Es hilft kein Wort. Es gibt nichts zu verstehen.
Von seinen Schultern fällt das müde Licht
Wie Staub. Er muß im Dunklen weitergehen.

DER FERNE FREUND

Ein Lebenslauf im Zeitraffer

Ein Dutzend Begegnungen
über Jahrzehnte verteilt
meist zwischen Tür und Angel

Einmal ein unglaubliches Treffen
in Santa Maria Maggiore
zufällig vor demselben
Regenguß fliehend

Einmal eine Postkarte:
die Chemotherapie
ist überstanden

Das Gesicht undeutlich
mit Bart und ohne

VII

LUIGI P.

Through empty parks, through lanes and avenues,
He's walking in the twilight, there he goes
Wrapped up in silence – every step he takes
Makes everything more alien. What is news?
He hesitates, looks shocked. Is this some joke?
Everyone passing by now seems to choose
Snow-white hair, and among them there are some
Looking like friends he was condemned to lose.
He's freezing, pulls his coat more tightly round him.
No words help. Unintelligible blues.
The weary light falls from his frame like dust.
He's got to walk on while the darkness grows.

YOUR DISTANT FRIEND

A life in quick motion

A dozen encounters
scattered across the decades
mostly just in passing

Once you improbably met
in Santa Maria Maggiore
escaping as it happened
from the very same cloudburst

Once a postcard:
my chemotherapy
has worked

His face indistinct
with a beard and without one

auf zerfließenden Fotos
am schärfsten im Traum –

Und plötzlich sitzt er
dir auf dem Sofa gegenüber

mit jeder Auferstehung

ein sichtbares Stück näher
dem Tod

EIN DICHTER STIRBT

1

Von aller Sprache
ist dir nur diese geblieben –

zuckende Schrift
auf dem Monitor

Ich lese sie
wie einst die
bläulichen Schwünge
deiner Handschrift –

(Mit wieviel Freude
entdeckte ich sie oft
von Regen Schnee verwischt
auf Briefen
im Postkasten)

Nun herrscht Reduktion:
drei Zeilen nur
Atem Herzschlag Körperwärme –

on dissolving photos
most clear-cut in your dreams –

Then all of a sudden he's sitting
there opposite you on the sofa

with every resurrection

a clear bit closer to
Death

A POET DIES

1

Of all your language
only this remains to you –

the convulsive script
on the monitor

I read it
as I did once
your handwriting's
bluish sweeps –

(With how much pleasure
I often discovered it
blurred by rain or snow
on letters
in the post-box)

Now reduction rules:
three lines only
breathing heart-beat body-heat –

doch fortgeschrieben
mit fiebriger Hast
als triebe sie
ein leuchtender Einfall
über jede Seite hinaus –

Manchmal plötzlich
springen Funken
Blitze
wie im Finale
eines Gedichts –

Eine Schwester kommt
drückt eine Taste
fixiert
deine blind
gestikulierende
Hand

2

Ich hatte nicht erwartet
sie noch einmal zu sehen –

doch sie kehren wieder
deine Augen

aus welcher Ferne
aus welchem Dickicht
aus welcher Wildnis –

Sie starren mich an
wild fremd

Vor meinen Worten
zucken sie zurück
wie vor einer
Mißhandlung

but written further
in feverish haste
as though some radiant thought
were impelling them
on, on, to the next page, on –

Sometimes all of a sudden
sparks leap
lightning-flashes strike
like in the finale
of a poem –

A nurse appears
presses a button
stares at
your blindly
gesticulating
hand

2

I'd not expected
to see them again –

but they return,
your eyes

from what distance
from what thicket
from what wasteland –

They stare at me
savage alien

From my words
they recoil
as though from an act
of maltreatment

NACH DEM TOD IHRES MANNES

Als sie zurückkehrte
ins leere Haus
war da kein Dach mehr
die Wände krümmten sich weg
der Boden stürzte
ohne Halt –

Besucher die jetzt kommen
führt sie durch weiße Zimmer
jeder Sessel und Tisch
jede Vase steht
im exakten Winkel
alle Bilder hängen
lotrecht
in diesem Haus in dem
die Gesetze der
Geometrie
nicht mehr gelten

STERBEGEDICHT ODER GESCHICHTE RÜCKWÄRTS

Wir können nichts mehr
für Sie tun
sagt das 21. Jahrhundert
im weißen Kittel
desinfiziert sich die Hände
und rollt die Geräte hinaus –
Das 19. singt zum Abschied
ein letztes Schubertlied
das 18. eine Bachkantate –
Dann geht alles sehr rasch:
Newton verliert seinen Apfel
Der Papst flieht aus der Stadt
Kolumbus segelt auf seiner
Santa Maria über den Rand
der Weltscheibe und stürzt

AFTER HER HUSBAND'S DEATH

When she went back
to the empty house
no roof was there
the walls cringed away
the floor collapsed
there was no holding it –

She leads her visitors now
through white rooms
every comfortable chair and table
every vase is at
just the right angle
all the pictures are hanging
in plumb
in this house in which
the laws of
geometry
don't any longer apply

FUNEREAL POEM OR HISTORY BACKWARDS

We can't do anything more
for you
says the 21st century
in its white smock
disinfects its hands
and rolls out the machines –
the 19th sings a last Schubert song
to bid you farewell
the 18th a cantata by Bach –
Then everything happens very fast:
Newton loses his apple
The pope flees from the city
Columbus sails in his
Santa Maria over the edge
of the flat world and plunges

ins Leere – was sonst?
Das Kreuzritterheer versinkt
im Morast
Dort hinten brennt Rom
dort die Bibliothek von Alexandria
dort Troja
Platon ruft noch im Fliehen
einen Satz
Der Turm von Babel kracht nieder –
Hiob röchelt –
Schon ist die Gegend
kalt und kahl:
nichts als die Dünenlandschaft
weißer Laken –
In prähistorischer Öde
ein einsamer Käfer
der einmal Mensch war
liegt auf dem Rücken
und rührt sich nicht mehr

SCHLAF IN CHINATOWN

Rastlos
unter der leichten Decke

Stimmengewirr
und Sirenengeheul
du weißt nicht
ob draußen
oder in dir

Träume
kurz aufflackernd
wie die falschen
Zehntausend-Dollar-Scheine
die man hier verbrennt
für die Toten

into emptiness – what else?
The army of crusaders sinks down
into the swamp
Back there Rome is burning
there the Alexandrian Library
there Troy in flames
Plato while fleeing calls out
one last sentence
The Tower of Babel comes crashing down –
We hear Job's death-rattle –
The region's already
cold and barren:
nothing but a dune-like landscape
of white winding-sheets –
In prehistoric desolation
a solitary beetle
once human
is lying on its back
no longer moving

SLEEPING IN CHINATOWN

Restless
underneath the light cover

Tangle of voices
and howl of sirens
you don't know
whether outside
or in you

Dreams
flaring briefly
like the forged
ten-thousand-dollar notes
they burn here
for the dead

GOTT MUSS ZUSEHEN

Wie es Morgen wird
und wieder Abend
wie das Licht wandert
über das unberührte Bett
Kleider Spielsachen
wie es Tag um Tag
dunkel wird und wieder hell
im Zimmer des Kindes
das spurlos verschwunden ist
seit zwölf Jahren

DIE HEILIGE

Höllenvisionen
Verzückung und Schrecken

Selbstgeißelungen
Nachtwachen bis zur
Erschöpfung

Ein Engel stieß ihr
so schreibt sie
eine goldene Lanze
ins Herz
glühend
und riß ihr die
Eingeweide heraus

Gibt es Worte für
die stillen Momente
wenn nur das Licht
durch den Obstgarten
fällt

und sie an Gott
nicht denken muß?

GOD MUST BE WATCHING

The way day breaks
and evening comes down again
the way light roams
across the untouched bed
clothes playthings
the way day after day
it grows dark and light again
in the room of the child
which vanished twelve years ago
without trace

THE SAINT

Hellish visions
transport and dread

Self-castigations
night-watches until her strength
is all spent

An angel – she writes –
plunged a
golden lance
into her heart
tipped with fire
and tore out
her bowels

Are there words for
those silent moments
when there's only light
falling
through the orchard

and she's no need
to think of God?

LES FLEURS DU MAL

Hochgezüchtete Gewächse:
das Tropenklima
muß stimmen
die Temperatur
darf nicht sinken –
nur in Treibhaus-
atmosphäre
und mit viel
Sorgfalt gedeihen
die Blumen des Bösen –

Anders die Blumen
des Guten:
ihr Blühen ist
anspruchslos
Hagelschauer Frost
bringen sie nicht um
und es bedarf
all unsrer Wachsamkeit
und Mühe
um ihr fragloses
Dasein
zu ersticken

GESTÄNDNIS

Vielleicht bei einem
Nachtgespräch
Auge in Auge
hättest auch du
dich von der seltsam
bildhaften Rede
dieses Mannes
dem alleserfaßenden
Lodern

LES FLEURS DU MAL

Mannered creations:
the tropical climate
has got to be right
the temperature
has not got to plummet –
only in a hot-house
atmosphere
and with a great deal of
care do the
flowers of evil
thrive –

The flowers of good
are different:
their blossoming's
unpretentious
hailstorms frost
don't do them in
and it requires
all our vigilance
and all our efforts
to snuff out
their questionless
existence

CONFESSION

Perhaps eye-to-eye
in the course of some
nightly conversation
perhaps you too
would have been set alight
by the curiously
figurative speech
of this man
by the ardour

seiner Forderung
in Brand
setzen lassen –

aber schon am
nächsten Morgen
wäre dir wieder
sehr viel verläßlicher
erschienen
der klare Verstand
und trockene Witz
des Pilatus

EPIPHANIE
nach einer Zeitungsmeldung

Kein oben und unten
im Universum
Keine Hierarchie
der Orte –

Der Sand vor Damaskus
nicht würdiger
als der Fleck auf einer
Pastetenpackung
in dem Janet McPherson
29jährige Britin
das Antlitz
Jesu Christi
erkennen will

of his demands
an ardour that
spreads to everything –

already though
on the following morning
you'd once again
have found
the clear logic
and dry wit
of Pilate
a good deal
more reliable

EPIPHANY
based on a newspaper story

No top no bottom
to the universe
No hierarchy
to separate places –

The sand near Damascus
no more worthy
than the speck on a
pasty package
in which 29-year-old Brit
Janet McPherson
claims she can
recognise
the face of Jesus Christ

GLAUBEN

Die Hand
ins Feuer legen –

Die Hand
die im Feuer liegt
so
oder so

VON DER UNBELEHRBARKEIT

Unser herrlicher Kosmos
so lehrt er
ist nur ein Schatten
ein Abbild –

Die Darmkoliken nehmen zu

Er will keine Spülungen
Arzneimittel keine Bäder

Nichts Dunkles ist im Geist
versteht ihr nicht?

Der Masseur stirbt
Die Angina wird bösartig
raubt ihm die Stimme
Eiter quillt aus seinem Körper

Die Schüler die er
mit einem Kuß begrüßt
bleiben weg vor Ekel

Er muß die Stadt verlassen
sich auf ein Landgut schleppen
Fieber schüttelt ihn

BELIEF

You put your hand into the fire
as Scaevola did –

Your hand
which is lying in the fire
whatever
you do

ON UNTEACHABLENESS

Our glorious cosmos
he teaches
is just a shadow
a copy –

More and more intestinal colics

He won't accept any irrigations
medicines baths

There's nothing dark in the mind
don't you see?

His masseur dies
his angina turns malignant
and robs him of his voice
pus pours from his body

The students he usually
greets with a kiss
stay away in disgust

He has to leave town
and drags himself to some country estate
in the grip of fever

Vier Mal im Leben gelang es mir
zu schauen –

Jetzt ist er nur noch
ein Haufen verwesender
Unrat

Jetzt spricht er nur noch
vom Licht

MAN SCHÄMT SICH ZU SAGEN

Und dann gibt es noch
eine andere Wahrheit
Eine Wahrheit die klein ist
Man schämt sich zu sagen
wie klein –

Die halbzerquetschte
Beere
die die Kinderhand
dir hinhält
ist groß dagegen

DIESES PRIVILEG...

Dieses Privileg
da zu sein
als Nachtfalter Iltis Molekül
als Stein oder Mensch
zwischen Abermilliarden
verworfener Möglichkeiten
ungezeugter Leben
da zu sein –

I managed four times in my life
to see –

Now he is only
a heap of
putrescence

Now he speaks only
about the light

ONE IS ASHAMED TO SAY

And then there's another
truth again
A small type of truth
One is ashamed to say
how small –

The half-squashed
berry
the child's hand
holds out to you
looks big by comparison

THIS PRIVILEGE...

This privilege
of being here
as a moth a polecat a molecule
as a stone or a man
of being here
in the midst of countless
rejected possibilities
of life untried –

reglos stumm
oder mit Atem
Herzschlag Schmerzempfinden
in hellen in dunklen Zimmern
zu kämpfen zu lieben
zu träumen oder
nicht weiter zu wissen
schlaflos zu liegen
zu hoffen daß die Zeit
vergeht

VERZÖGERTE POST

Der Jüngste Tag
das wird
der Tag sein an dem
alle je an uns gerichteten
und noch vor
der Absendung zerrissenen
Briefe
alle durchgestrichenen
Zeilen und nur
erdachten Sätze
bei uns eintreffen werden
auf einen Schlag

DANKESBRIEF AN MR LAUREL UND MR HARDY

Seit früher Kindheit
zähle ich auf euch
auf die glänzende Zuversicht
eurer schwarzen Melonen
die ihr selbst im Taifun
nie verliert –

motionless mute
or drawing breath
with a beating heart an awareness of pain
in bright in dark rooms
destined to fight to love
to dream or
to be at a loss
to lie there unable to sleep
to hope that time
will fly past

POST DELIVERED LATE

The Last Judgement
that will be
the day on which
all letters ever
meant for us
but torn up
before they were sent
all cancelled
lines and
merely conceived-of sentences
reach us
at one fell stroke

LETTER OF THANKS TO MR LAUREL AND MR HARDY

Since earliest childhood
I've counted on you
on the shiny assurance
of your black bowlers
which you never lose
not even in a typhoon –

Vor aller Philosophie
habt ihr mir
die Welt erklärt –

Ehern der kategorische
Imperativ der euch befiehlt
Weihnachtsbäume zu verkaufen
im Hochsommer
oder mit Kontrabaß und Harmonium
ein Konzert zu geben
vor einer Taubstummenanstalt –

Im aufgeräumtesten
Frühlingsmorgen
entfacht ihr unweigerlich
das dialektische Streichholz
daß euch und uns
die Fetzen
samt Gasherd und Teekanne
um die
Ohren fliegen –

Homo homini lupus –
wer zweifelt,
zwischen schießwütigen Gattinnen
und cholerischen Schankkellnern?

Und doch überbietet ihr Leibniz
mit eurem Optimismus
wenn ihr
nichts in der Tasche als
einen falschen Tausender
im Grandhotel
das beste aller möglichen
Diners bestellt –

Klarer als Schopenhauer
seht ihr:

before all philosophy
you explained
the world to me –

Iron-clad the categorical
imperative commanding you
to sell Christmas trees
at the height of summer
or with a double-bass and a harmonium
to give a concert
to a home for the deaf and dumb –

On the very most jovial
spring morning
you can be depended upon to light
the dialectical match
causing all
along with the gas-stove
and teapot
to explode in your faces and ours

Homo homini lupus –
who doubts it
there between trigger-happy wives
and choleric barkeepers?

And yet you outdo Leibnitz
with your optimism
when with nothing
in your pocket
but a forged thousand-buck note
you order the best of all possible
dinners in the grand hotel –

More clearly than Schopenhauer
you see:

das Leben ist eine
morsche Hängebrücke
über die man
betrunken
einen Klavier schieben muß
während von drüben
ein wütender Gorilla
entgegenkommt –

Wenn ihr mich nicht hinüberstoßt
hinüberschleift
kopfüber kopfunter
mit Hängen und Würgen –

Platon
schafft es gewiß nicht

life is a
rotten suspension bridge
across which drunk
you must push a piano
while from the other side

a furious gorilla
is lumbering towards you –

If you can't push me over
or else drag me over
head first or feet first
by the skin of my teeth –

Plato
certainly won't manage

VIII

EINEM JUNGEN ELTERNPAAR

Und plötzlich
kann man sie auch
an euch entdecken:

diese merkwürdig
unbeholfene
stockende Gangart
all derer
denen ihr Herz
immer um einige
Meter
voraus-
läuft

STIMMEN, LAUTE

Jeder Satz den wir
sprechen
gleichgültig, beim Abendessen –

Für dich ein Raunen
orphisches Urwort
geheimnisvolle
Offenbarung –

Alles geht dich an
hat Bedeutung –

Erst nach und nach
wirst du dich
(wie wir uns nach
einem Konzert

VIII

TO A YOUNG MOTHER AND FATHER

And all
of a sudden
you've got it too:

the oddly
heavy-footed
faltering gait
of all
whose heart
is yards
in front of them
running a-
head

VOICES, SOUNDS

Every sentence that we
speak,
indifferent, at supper –

For you it's a charm,
it's orphic,
a cryptic
revelation –

Everything concerns you,
has import –

Only by and by
will you
(as we do after
a concert,

einem langen Flug
einer Umarmung)
zögernd
einfinden
in die Welt
des Banalen

PANIK
als wir ahnungslos in eine Oper gingen,
in der der Bombenangriff auf Dresden mit Tönen simuliert wurde

Der Bunker aus Fleisch und Blut
die pulsenden Mauern
um dich:
sterblicher Schutz der
kein Schutz ist –

Wußten wir es nicht?

Alles trifft dich:
selbst das Schrillen der Bomben
einer längst vergangenen Nacht –

Ich denke an die Frau
die sagte sie hätte
nichts tun können
damals in Dresden
als ihrem Kind
die Augen die
Ohren zuhalten –

Wie sollen wir dich
schützen
angstvolles Herz
im Dunklen
mit unseren Händen –

a long flight,
an embrace)
take your hesitant
place
in the nether world
of banality

PANIC

when we went unsuspectingly to an opera
where the bombing of Dresden was simulated by musical means

The bunker of flesh and blood
the throbbing walls
around you:
mortal protection which
is no protection –

Didn't we get it?

Everything hits you:
even the shriek of bombs
dropped on a long-gone night –

I think of the woman
who said she'd been
powerless to act
back then in Dresden
except to stop up
her child's ears
and eyes –

How should we
protect you
anxious heart
in the dark with our hands –

Noch durch unsere
fest zusammen-
gepreßten Finger
schießt sie dir
gewaltsam
entgegen:
unsre Welt

ES IST SOWEIT

Der weißgekachelte Raum
hat keine Fenster

Deine Mutter
unterm Flügelhemd nackt
rasiert
mit einer Kanüle

Als gäbe es plötzlich
nur noch sie und mich –

Unsre Blicke
brennen
wie in der ersten Umarmung

wenn wir uns ansehn
über der zuckenden
Nadel
des Wehenschreibers

Through our tightly
closed fingers
it's still shooting
violently
towards you:
this world of ours

IT'S TIME

The white-tiled room
is windowless

Your mother
naked beneath her
operation shirt
shaved
and trailing a cannula

As though there were suddenly
only her and me in the world –

Our looks
burn
like in our first embrace

as we gaze at one other
above the convulsive
needle
busy writing up her contractions

AUF MEINEM SCHOSS

Meine Tochter schreibt

Ihr Stift gräbt Runen
Keilschrift
Hieroglyphen

Zu Stein wird ihr Gesicht
Ihre Augen
verwandeln sich in
blaue Skarabäen

Unnahbar sitzt sie
mit Sphinxschultern
mit Pythiamund

und gräbt und gräbt
Zeichen um Zeichen

jedes bedeutet die Welt

das Blatt zerreißt
unter der Gewalt

Sie sieht es nicht
fühlt nicht mein Streicheln

ihr Name rieselt
von ihrem Haar
als Wüstensand

ON MY LAP

My daughter is writing

Her pen carves out runes
cuneiform letters
hieroglyphs

Her face turns to stone
Her eyes
into blue
scarabaeuses

Unapproachable she's sitting
with sphinx's shoulders
a Pythia's mouth

and carving out carving out
sign after sign

each of them signifies the world

the paper tears
beneath this brute force

She doesn't see it
doesn't feel me caressing her

her name sifts
off her hair
as desert sand

NOTES

p. 29 'Aristotle thought…': An allusion to the dichotomy which Aristotle postulates between form and matter – fossils as an error of nature.

p. 33 'Nada': "Forest paths" is an attempt to paraphrase the German term "Holzweg" – literally a woodland path, although "auf einem Holzweg sein" means "to be on the wrong path" / "to be barking up the wrong tree" in everyday German. The poet is clearly alluding, beyond this, to Martin Heidegger's book of essays *Holzwege* – explorations which resemble "Wege, die meist verwachsen jäh im Unbegangenen aufhören" (paths which mostly end abruptly, overgrown, in untrodden parts), to quote Heidegger's preface.

p. 61 'Places': From 1905 onwards, the Austrian poet Georg Trakl (1887-1914) served an apprenticeship at this chemist's in Salzburg, then called "The White Angel" (Zum Weißen Engel). One reason Trakl chose the profession of dispensing chemist was to be in the vicinity of drugs. His death, induced by his despair at having to treat wounded soldiers without anaesthetics after the Battle of Grodek, was due to an overdose of cocaine.

p. 63 'Biographies': Steinherr alludes in the various strophes, in turn, to the German expressionist poet Georg Heym (who drowned in an ice-skating accident), to the Czech writer Bohumil Hrabal (who fell out of a fifth-floor window while feeding pigeons), to the Austrian playwright and novelist Ödön von Horváth (who was slain by a branch on a stormy night), and to the American novelist Sherwood Anderson (who died of peritonitis brought on by swallowing a toothpick in an *hors d'oeuvre*).

p. 63 'Inside the books…': "the rumble of guns outside Jena" alludes to Hegel writing his *Phenomenology of Mind* in 1806 as a battle raged. Hegel plays a prominent role in Steinherr's philosophy (*cf.* his dissertation, which is an attempt to "build a bridge" between Hegel and Quine, e-mail of 15 November 2004), but this is a rare reference in a poem. "This is what always happens to me when I connect Hegel with literature: either I'd have to say far too much – or I can't say anything. This is why my favourite philosopher hardly appears in my poetry, although I keep giving space to other thinkers. Hegel is simply too complex, too easily misunderstood, and above all too heavily distorted by traditional interpretations. In a certain sense, I am a Hegelian – but a Hegelian who distrusts the concept of systems. A Hegelian who doesn't wish to be linked either with the right or the left wing of the movement, a Hegelian who is dubious about Hegelianism in general." (e-mail of 5 November 2005).

p. 73 'An early representation of Adam and Eve': Inspired by the eleventh-century representation of the expulsion of Adam and Eve from paradise on a bronze panel in Hildesheim Cathedral (see cover).

p. 85 'Death of the Painter': Velasquéz.

p. 91 'Second': Sei Shonagan (966/7-1013?) was a Japanese writer and courtesan; Steinherr is alluding to *The Pillow Book of Sei Shonagan* (996).

p. 91 'On a photo of Franziska zu Reventlow': Franziska Countess Reventlow (1871-1918) was a writer and also a prominent figure in bohemian Munich circles for more than a decade from 1892 onwards.

p. 95 'Original beneath all the copies': An allusion to the Platonic theory. *Cf.* E.H. Gombrich, *Art and Illusion,* 5th edition, London 1977, p. 83: "There are few more influential discussions on the philosophy of representation than the momentous passage in the *Republic* where Plato introduces the comparison between a painting and a mirror image. It has haunted the philosophy of art ever since. To re-examine his theory of ideas, Plato contrasts the painter with the carpenter. The carpenter who makes the couch translates the idea, or concept, of the couch into matter. The painter who represents the carpenter's couch in one of his paintings only copies the appearance of one particular couch. He is thus twice removed from the idea."

p. 99 'On the unconcerned world': The coach-trip is the eerily funereal one which the heroine takes with her undependable lover Léon through the streets of Rouen in *Madame Bovary.*

p. 105 'Homo sapiens': Porphyry speaks in his introduction to Aristotle's *Categories* of man being defined as the animal capable of laughter.

p. 105 'A disquisition on the human spirit': Refers to a report on a man kept hostage for years by a liberation organisation.

p. 109 'Lago di Tovel': Steinherr's vision has been darkened by his awareness of ubiquitous violence; the red tint which used to often be noticed in the waters of the Lago di Tovel in northern Italy was caused by the presence of certain algae.

p. 117 'Luigi P.': Pirandello, incidentally the subject of a key early poem by Steinherr.

p. 127 'The saint': Teresa of Avila.

p. 133 'Belief': The play on words in this poem evades translation. The German idiom "die Hand ins Feuer legen" (literally "to put one's hand in the fire") implies vouching for somebody or something, "putting oneself on the line".

p. 133 'On unteachableness': A crystallisation of the life and work of Plotinus.

Ludwig Steinherr was born in Munich in 1962, where he still lives, and studied philosophy at the University of Munich (writing an M.A. thesis on Hegel's *Wissenschaft der Logik* and a much-noted doctorate on Hegel and Quine, *"Holismus, Existenz und Identität". Ein systematischer Vergleich zwischen Quine und Hegel*). He is now a free-lance writer and lecturer in philosophy at the University of Eichstätt.

Steinherr has worked as an essayist, a reviewer, a juror, a translator (of Michael Hamburger, among others), and as an editor, co-founding the influential journal *Das Gedicht* with Anton G. Leitner in 1993. But it is as a poet that he has written his way into the front rank of contemporary German writers, one milestone here being the selection of his poem 'Sage' (Legend) as "Gedicht des Jahres" (Poem of the Year) by the Autoreninitiative Köln in 1987. The present volume has been selected from his first ten collections, beginning with his 1985 debut volume, *Fluganweisung* (Flight Instructions), up to *Die Hand im Feuer* (The Hand in the Fire), 2005; since then he has published two further poetry collections, *Von Stirn zu Gestirn* (From Brow to Constellation) in 2007 and *Kometenjagd* (Hunting for Comets) in 2009.

Steinherr's poems have also been published widely in magazines and anthologies in Germany and abroad – in Raymond Hargreaves' *Young Poets of Germany* (Forest Books, 1994), for instance, and in the 1994 *Agenda* German Issue, edited by Michael Hamburger and Richard Dove – and have received a number of awards, including the Leonce-und-Lena-Förderpreis (1993), the Buchpreis des Verbandes Evangelischer Büchereien (1999) and the Hermann-Hesse-Förderpreis (1999). They have also been translated into various languages, including French and Czech.

Steinherr was elected a fellow of the Bayerische Akademie der Schönen Künste (Bavarian Academy of Fine Arts) in 2003.

Richard Dove was born in Bath in 1954, read Modern Languages at Oxford and taught German and English language and literature at the Universities of Exeter, Regensburg and Wales before moving to Munich in

1987, where he has since worked as a writer and lecturer. His early poems were recently collected in the bilingual volume *Aus einem früheren Leben* (From an Earlier Life. Lyrikedition, 2000, 2003), translated *inter alia* by Hans Magnus Enzensberger and Reiner Kunze. Since moving to Germany, he has written his poems very largely in German: *Farbfleck auf einem Mondrian-Bild. Gedichte* (Speck of Paint on a Mondrian. Poems. Edition Thaleia, 2002); *Am Fluß der Wohlgerüche. Gedichte* (By the Fragrant River. Poems. Rimbaud Verlag, 2008); and *Syrische Skyline. Gedichte* (Syrian Skyline. Poems. Rimbaud Verlag, 2009). He also translates into English.

Apart from this Steinherr selection, Dove has published versions of poems by Michael Krüger, *Diderot's Cat. Selected Poems* (Diderots Katze. Ausgewählte Gedichte. Carcanet, 1993 / Braziller, 1994) and *At Night, Beneath Trees* (Nachts, Unter Bäumen. Braziller 1998); Ernst Meister, *Not Orpheus. Selected Poems* (Nicht Orpheus. Ausgewählte Gedichte. Carcanet, 1996); Friederike Mayröcker, *Raving Language. Selected Poems 1946-2006* (Rasende Sprache. Ausgewählte Gedichte. Carcanet, 2007), and others. His editions include a bilingual collection by Joachim Sartorius, *Ice Memory. Selected Poems* (Carcanet, 2006), translated *inter alia* by Robert Gray, Michael Hamburger, Christopher Middleton, Nathaniel Tarn and Rosmarie Waldrop.

JEAN BOASE-BEIER was born in Huddersfield in 1954, and studied at the universities of Manchester and Regensburg. She taught Linguistics and German in Regensburg before moving to the University of East Anglia in 1991, where she is Professor of Literature and Translation. She has translated Ernst Meister and (with Anthony Vivis) Rose Ausländer for Arc Pub-lications, and has published widely on stylistics and literary translation.

Also available in the Arc Publications
'VISIBLE POETS' SERIES (Series Editor: Jean Boase-Beier)

No. 1 – MIKLÓS RADNÓTI (Hungary)
Camp Notebook
Translated by Francis Jones, introduced by George Szirtes

No. 2 – BARTOLO CATTAFI (Italy)
Anthracite
Translated by Brian Cole, introduced by Peter Dale
(Poetry Book Society Recommended Translation)

No. 3 – MICHAEL STRUNGE (Denmark)
A Virgin from a Chilly Decade
Translated by Bente Elsworth, introduced by John Fletcher

No. 4 – TADEUSZ RÓZEWICZ (Poland)
recycling
Translated by Barbara Bogoczek (Plebanek) & Tony Howard,
introduced by Adam Czerniawski

No. 5 – CLAUDE DE BURINE (France)
Words Have Frozen Over
Translated by Martin Sorrell, introduced by Susan Wicks

No. 6 – CEVAT ÇAPAN (Turkey)
Where Are You, Susie Petschek?
Translated by Cevat Çapan & Michael Hulse,
introduced by A. S. Byatt

No. 7 – JEAN CASSOU (France)
33 Sonnets of the Resistance
With an original introduction by Louis Aragon
Translated by Timothy Adès, introduced by Alistair Elliot

No. 8 – ARJEN DUINKER (Holland)
The Sublime Song of a Maybe
Translated by Willem Groenewegen, introduced by Jeffrey
Wainwright

No. 9 – MILA HAUGOVÁ (Slovakia)
Scent of the Unseen
Translated by James & Viera Sutherland-Smith,
introduced by Fiona Sampson

No. 10 – ERNST MEISTER (Germany)
Between Nothing and Nothing
Translated by Jean Boase-Beier, introduced by John Hartley Williams

No. 22 – FERNANDO KOFMAN (Argentina)
The Flights of Zarza
Translated by Ian Taylor, introduced by Andrew Graham Yooll

No. 23 – LARISSA MILLER (Russia)
Guests of Eternity
Translated by Richard McKane, introduced by Sasha Dugdale
(Poetry Book Society Recommended Translation)

No. 24 – ANISE KOLTZ (Luxembourg)
At the Edge of Night
Translated by Anne-Marie Glasheen, introduced by Caroline Price

No. 25 – MAURICE CARÊME (Belgium)
Defying Fate
Translated by Christopher Pilling, introduced by Martin Sorrell

No. 26 – VALÉRIE ROUZEAU (France)
Cold Spring in Winter
Translated by Susan Wicks, introduced by Stephen Romer
(Short-listed, Griffin Poetry Prize, 2010 &
Oxford-Weidenfeld Translation Prize, 2010)

No. 27 – RAZMIK DAVOYAN (France)
Whispers and Breath of the Meadows
Translated by Arminé Tamrazian, introduced by W. N. Herbert

No. 28 – FRANÇOIS JACQMIN (Belgium)
The Book of the Snow
Translated by Philip Mosley, introduced by Clive Scott

No. 29 – KRISTIINA EHIN (Estonia)
The Scent of Your Shadow
Translated by Ilmar Lehtpere, introduced by Sujata Bhatt
(Poetry Book Society Recommended Translation)

No. 30 – META KUŠAR (Slovenia)
Ljubljana
Translated by Ana Jelnikar & Stephen Watts, introduced by Francis R. Jones